STORAGE 1-6

CONTENTS

THE BOOK

THERE WAS SOMETHING ABOUT THE SMELL AFTER A SUDDEN rainstorm that made Jack Harkness think of death. He struggled to think of the exact memory this might be attached to, whatever moment in his long and eventful past that may have involved a rainstorm and a death, but there it was, deep in his subconscious. Today was no different.

The SUV was parked up alongside a caravan, in the centre of a vast park full of near-identical mobile homes. Gwen was sat inside the SUV, her arm around a crying young woman named Kelly Jenkins. Owen and Tosh were inside the caravan itself. Jack would have to go back inside soon enough, though he wasn't sure he could bear it.

Owen emerged from the caravan, his hand over his mouth. His and Jack's eyes met, and Owen shook his head.

"Seriously," he said, "That is some messed up stuff in there. I mean... Literally. If I wasn't technically dead I'd have thrown up by now. We're gonna have to use DNA to get a positive ID. I'd have suggested dental records but... well... even his teeth are all over the place."

"It's Frank," said Jack.

"Are you sure?"

"Pretty sure."

Owen gestured toward the SUV with a nod.

"That's the missus, then?"

Jack nodded.

Owen looked through the darkened windows of the SUV, and raised an appreciative eyebrow.

"Well, this Frank fella had good taste in birds. And an eye for the younger lady. Trophy wife, was she?"

Jack laughed wistfully.

"Something like that," he said.

"So who was he?" Owen asked.

"Frank Jenkins?" said Jack, "Frank Jenkins was a Jack of all trades. Former marine. Served in the Falklands. He was a mercenary in the mid '80s. Fought in Nigeria, El Salvadore. All the fun places. Then in about '87 he set up shop as a salesman."

"Double-glazing?"

"Artefacts."

Owen nodded sagely.

"Oh..."

"Exactly. That's when he first appears on our files. Frank might have had somebody working inside Torchwood. We never really got to the bottom of it. If you were a collector of alien artefacts, Frank Jenkins was the guy to go to. Henry Parker was almost certainly a client of his, as was Cybil Rothman."

"That mad old spinster who collected Weevil skulls?"

"That's the one. She was buying off Frank from the start."

"Well, Parker was clean. Nuts but clean. Do you think this could be connected to Rothman?" asked Owen.

"Possibly," Said Jack. "But she's dead now, just like Parker. Not many of the old fashioned collectors left now. End of an era," he sighed, wistfully.

It was only a few weeks since Torchwood had encountered Cybil Rothman. The last in line of a great banking dynasty, she had breathed her last in a crumbling mansion just outside the city. In the days following her death, Torchwood had searched the house to find it full of artefacts that had no place being there.

"Surely she wasn't mixed up in anything like *this*, though?" asked Owen.

Before Jack could answer his question they were joined by Ianto, carrying four cups of coffee in a cardboard tray, and a paper bag. He was whistling Oh, I Do Love To Be Beside The Seaside, but stopped abruptly when both Jack and Owen shot him icy glares.

"What's in the bag?" asked Owen.

"Doughnuts," said Ianto, slightly out of breath from the uphill walk from the seafront to the caravan park. "Can't have a cup of coffee at the seaside without a doughnut."

"Have you *been* in there?" said Owen, pointing at the caravan with his thumb, "I don't think Tosh is gonna be very peckish when she comes out."

OF JAHI

PART 1

BY DAVID LLEWELLYN

ILLUSTRATIONS MIKE DOWLING

"Oh," said Ianto, wincing, "Like that, is it?"

Owen nodded gravely. He looked in through the windows of the SUV once more. The young blonde was still crying, her mascara forming messy black trails down her cheeks.

"Poor thing," he said, "As if living *here* wasn't bad enough."

Ianto put the coffees and the bag of doughnuts on the bonnet of the SUV.

"I don't know," he said, "It's not that bad. We used to come here all the time when I was a kid."

"Yeah, back when it was a holiday park," said Owen. "Now it's a bloody shanty town."

Owen was right. Though there was little to distinguish Sunny Bay Caravan Park from any other holiday resort on first sight, it soon became apparent that the inhabitants were not on holiday. It was in their faces, and the way they carried themselves. Each and every one of them was little more than a refugee, temporarily housed there after being forcibly evicted from their homes in Cwmblaidd. The town they had thought of as home would, within 24 hours, be submerged beneath a vast reservoir, the largest hydroelectric facility in Europe. Whatever sentimental attachment they may have had to the bricks and mortar around them stood for little against the march of progress and commerce.

"So," said Ianto, nodding in the direction of Gwen and Kelly, "has she said anything yet?"

"I don't think so," said Jack. "What can she say? She came home to find her husband dead – and not just murdered... I'm not even sure what kind of weapon could do that to a person."

Owen grimaced. ▶

"Please, Jack, don't remind me."

The door of the SUV opened and Gwen stepped out. She took a deep breath and sighed.

"She okay?" said Jack.

"Well," said Gwen, "not really, Jack, no. She said she'd like to speak to you, though."

Jack nodded and walked past the others to climb into the SUV. Inside, Kelly, a beautiful young woman no older than 25, sat with her head in her hands.

"Hey," said Jack, softly. "I'm Jack Harkness. I know this is a difficult time, but there are a few questions I'd like to ask, if that's okay."

Kelly looked up at Jack with bloodshot eyes and nodded, sniffing.

"Okay," said Jack, "Kelly, did Frank ever talk about a woman called Cybil Rothman? Did he ever mention that name?"

Kelly paused, wiping her nose with a handkerchief. She breathed in and composed herself.

"I don't know," she said. "I'm not sure. Who is she?"

"A rich old lady," said Jack. "Lived in a great big mansion not far from here. Frank might have worked for her. We're not sure just yet."

"What was her name again?"

"Cybil Rothman."

Kelly paused once more, her brow furrowed in concentration.

"It's familiar," she said. "I know the name from somewhere. Wait..."

Her eyes opened wider and she started nodding slowly.

"Yeah," she said. "Razors. Razors worked for her."

"Razors?" said Jack.

"Yeah," said Kelly. "Razors Maguire. He was an old army mate of Frank's. He used to run a security company, years ago. I'm sure he said something about working for this old woman. Said she never left the house. Like that woman in Great Expectations. Weird old thing, he said."

"Razors Maguire?" Jack asked. "That's his real name?"

Kelly laughed softly, tears still streaming down her cheeks.

"No," she said. "No, his real name's Doug. Everyone just calls him Razors. He lives in Cardiff. Do you think he's got something to do with... with *this*?"

She looked out through the windows at the caravan. Following her gaze Jack saw blood on a curtain. Kelly started sobbing again.

"No," said Jack. "I don't think so. But we might need to speak to him. Maybe he can help us find out."

Kelly nodded.

Jack put his hand on her shoulder and looking at her with a sympathetic smile squeezed it gently.

"Thank you, Kelly," he said. "You've been more than helpful. We'll make sure there's somewhere for you to stay tonight. Do you have family at all?"

Kelly shook her head.

"No," she said, still sobbing, "there was only Frank."

Jack nodded. Taking his hand away from her shoulder he opened the door and stepped back outside.

"Okay," he said to the team. "Ianto, I need you to find somewhere for Kelly to stay. Maybe one of the safe houses. But somewhere nice, okay? Owen, you and Tosh need to clean up in there and search everything, and I mean *everything*. Gwen, you and I need to speak to a man named Razors Maguire."

Gwen looked at Jack, startled.

"Razors?" she said. "Razors Maguire?"

"Yeah. You know him?"

"Know *of* him," said Gwen. "And let's just say he's not named after his mobile phone."

The clouds were beginning to part and slivers of bright sunshine spilled over the western edges of the city as Jack and Gwen pulled up outside a block of flats. It was an ugly monolith of a building, eight storeys tall, flanked on each side by similarly brutal, featureless slabs. It seemed that half of the windows in each building were covered with metal screens. A nearby phonebox stood, no more than a metal frame, the ground around it covered in countless fragments of shattered glass. Next to the phonebox, a car perched on stacked bricks; the wheels gone, and the driver's side window punched through. Inside was a gaping hole where the stereo should have been.

"Nice," said Jack. "I like what they've done with the place."

Moments later they were climbing the stairs to the sixth floor of the building. There had been 'OUT OF ORDER' signs on all of the elevator doors, in a lobby that smelled distinctly unpleasant. The stairwell around them was sprayed

liberally with graffiti and littered with discarded bottles and cans. When they eventually reached the door to Razors Maguire's flat they pressed the doorbell and waited.

After an age the door opened on a short chain, and a face appeared in the narrow gap between the door and the frame.

Razors Maguire stood there in a white vest and tracksuit trousers, his head shaved almost to the scalp, a tattoo of a bluebird on the side of his neck, and a cigarette hanging from one corner of his mouth.

"Who're you?" he grunted. "Police?"

Jack shook his head.

"We're Torchwood," he said.

"Never heard of you," said Maguire.

"We're here to talk about Frank Jenkins," interrupted Gwen.

"Oh yeah?" said Maguire, taking a long drag on his cigarette and blowing the smoke out into her face. "Wharrabout him?"

"He's dead," said Jack. "Murdered."

There was a long pause. Maguire's mean expression faded very quickly, and his shoulders slumped.

"Murdered?" he said, in disbelief. "By who?"

"We were hoping you might be able to help us," said Jack. "If we could just have a moment of your time. We can either do that here, or we can take you in."

Maguire sneered at them both and laughed through his nose.

"Aw, is it?" he said. "Gorra warrant for my arrest, have you?"

"We don't need one," said Jack, coldly. "We're not the police. And you *have* heard of us, haven't you, Razors?"

Maguire took one last drag on his cigarette and flicked it out into the corridor, where it lay smouldering on the tiled floor. With a disgruntled huff he unchained the door and opened it.

"You berra come in," he said. "Sorry about the mess."

As Jack and Gwen entered the flat they were both struck by the smell of takeaway food and cigarette smoke. Passing the kitchen they saw a sink filled with soiled plates and cups and work surfaces covered in coffee stains and breadcrumbs. The living room was a mess of overflowing ashtrays, empty beer cans, and random items of clothing strewn over every piece of furniture.

"Siddown," grunted Maguire, gesturing toward a threadbare sofa as he dropped himself down into a mismatched armchair.

Moving a pile of clothes and magazines to the floor, Jack and Gwen sat.

"So," said Maguire, "Whaddayou wanna know?"

"Cybil Rothman," said Jack, "You used to work for her?"

Maguire nodded.

"Used to, yeah," he said, "Coupla years ago, like. I was runnin' this security firm after I got out of prison. Interesting old bird. Why? What's this gorra do with Frank?"

"Cybil Rothman died a few weeks ago," said Gwen. "She was very old. But now Frank's been murdered..."

"Well I haven't worked for Cybil Rothman in years," said Maguire. "My firm went belly up and she hired somebody else. Then I worked as a bouncer for a bit. Remember the Hippo Club? Down on Penarth Road? I worked there until they closed that place. Been on disability ever since. Sciatica. I'm a martyr to my lower back, I swear."

Gwen nodded, trying her best to look sympathetic.

"Okay," she said. "When was the last time you saw Frank?"

Maguire frowned, taking another cigarette from a crumpled pack and lighting it.

"I dunno," he said. "Bout six weeks ago? He was moving out of his place in the valleys where they're building that reservoir. Him and the missus was quite upset about it."

"And did he talk about anything else? Did he mention anyone else?"

Maguire paused, blew out a plume of smoke, and nodded.

"Yeah," he said. "Yeah... He said he thought he was being followed."

Jack leaned forward. They were onto something, he could sense it.

"Really? By who?"

"Mr Glee," said Maguire, laughing nervously.

"Mr Glee?" said Jack, shooting a brief look at Gwen, who had shifted uneasily at the name.

"Yeah," said Maguire. "Loada nonsense if you ask me. I mean... Everyone's heard of Mr Glee, but nobody's ever seen 'im."

"He definitely said it was Mr Glee?" asked Gwen.

"Yeah," said Maguire, "but I reckoned he was just paranoid. Musta been the stress. You know, with them moving house and everything."

"I'm sorry," said Jack, "but who is Mr Glee?" ▶

"You never heard of Mr Glee?" said Maguire. "Everyone knows about Mr Glee!"

Jack shook his head and turned to Gwen.

"Have you?" he asked.

"A little," said Gwen. "When I was still on the force. We always thought it was somebody's cover."

"Well you mighta been right," said Maguire. "Like I says, nobody's ever seen 'im. I reckons you're about as likely to find Mr Glee as you are to find the flippin' Tooth Fairy."

"Okay," said Jack, getting to his feet. "Well, Razors... You've been very helpful."

"Goin' already?" said Maguire. "Not gonna stay for a brew?"

Gwen thought about the sink full of dirty cups and the stained work surfaces, and shook her head.

"No," she said, smiling politely, "we'd best be going."

Maguire followed them to the door. As they stepped out into the corridor and made their way toward the stairs, he leaned out through the doorway.

"Nice meeting you," he called, without a shred of sincerity.

Jack and Gwen were out of the building and halfway across the car park when they noticed that somebody, in the short time they had been inside, had sprayed a four-letter obscenity on the side of the SUV.

"Well that's just *great*," said Jack.

"At least they spelled it correctly," said Gwen. "I mean, they could have spelled it with a 'k'."

They climbed inside, and Jack paused for a moment before starting the engine.

"You think there's anything in this Mr Glee story?" he asked.

Gwen shrugged.

"Could be," she said. "I could always have a word with Andy. Like Razors said, he might just be a myth."

"Yeah," said Jack, as they pulled away from the kerb. "And maybe he's not."

Maguire watched them drive away from his window on the seventh floor, following them with his gaze until they had pulled out onto Cowbridge Road and vanished from sight.

Stubbing out his cigarette in an ashtray already filled with scrunched up butts he dropped back down into his armchair and turned on the television. He had been watching Cash In The Attic for no more than five minutes when his doorbell rang.

What had they come back for? Some Columbo-style "one more thing", before dragging him to their police station, or whatever it was Torchwood had? Swearing and grumbling under his breath he stood up, the sound of a fist impatiently thudding on the door as he walked.

"Hang on!" yelled Maguire, his slippers flapping against the linoleum in the hallway. "I'm comin'!"

He slid the chain into place, and opened his door, but before he could see who was there the door had been kicked wide open, the chain snapping out of its lock.

Maguire was struck across the face and knocked to the ground. Through blurred vision and a blizzard of colours he saw the dark shapes of his intruders bearing down on him, just before he was blindfolded and knocked unconscious by another blow.

"Y ou know something?" said Owen, taking down the blood-soaked curtains and dropping them into a yellow plastic bag.

"What's that?" said Toshiko. She was stood at the far end of the caravan's living room, dressed from head to toe in a forensic suit, searching through the items on a shelf filled with books, CDs and DVDs.

"I reckon if you were to tell somebody what we do for a living, I mean just open up and tell them, they'd probably think it was really cool and exciting and glamorous. And yet here we are..."

He picked up something small, red and wet from a window ledge. Through the rubber gloves it was impossible to properly feel its texture. He held it over the yellow bag for a moment, shook his head, and placed it instead into the large plastic container which held the rest of Frank Jenkins' remains.

"We get all the good jobs, don't we?" said Toshiko, looking over at him with a smile. "Me and you?"

"Yeah," sighed Owen. "If there's a limb to be retrieved from a storm drain or a gelatinous blob to be scraped off a ceiling, I'm your man. Found anything interesting in the DVDs? Any saucy home videos?"

"Not really," said Toshiko. "Looks like Kelly's a big fan of Reese Witherspoon and Frank was addicted to war films. I guess it's true what they say. You know... how opposites attract..."

She looked over at Owen, hoping he might look back at her, but he was too engrossed in his cleaning. Now that the sun was shining once more, the whole caravan had begun to feel like an oven, especially with them wearing overalls over their normal clothes. Somewhere in the room she could hear the buzzing of flies.

Sighing gently she returned her attention to the shelves, pulling plastic cases out one by one and checking them.

Sweet Home Alabama, Tora! Tora! Tora!, Legally Blonde 2, Saving Private Ryan... Then she came to a case with a blank spine. She pulled it off the shelf and gazed down at the cover.

"Er, Owen..." she said.

"Oh God," said Owen with disgust, holding up something which looked like a finger and grimacing at it before turning to face her. "Yes?"

"You might want to see this..."

Owen put down the yellow bag and crossed the room. As he drew nearer to her Toshiko held up the black plastic case. Tucked into the transparent outer cover of the case there was a scrap of paper on which was written just two words: '*FOR TORCHWOOD*'.

Razors Maguire was woken by the sudden sensation of ice cold water on his face. He was lying on his side on a cold cement floor in a room illuminated by a single bare bulb. Two men stood over him, both with shaved heads, both wearing near-matching black leather jackets. He thought he recognized them but it was hard to tell in this dim light, and with his one eye swollen shut.

The men held him by the arms and lifted him to his feet, dragging him from the small, featureless grey room and out into a long, dark corridor. Over and over again he asked them where he was and what they were going to do to him, but neither man spoke.

Eventually they came to a second room where the cuffs binding Maguire's wrists were slung around a hook in the centre of the ceiling, so that he hung there, his feet barely touching the ground. Another single bulb provided the only light in the room, channelled by a tin lampshade into a circular pool on the floor. As Maguire came to his senses he saw, at the edge of the shadows, the seated, half-hidden figure of a man in an expensive-looking pinstripe suit. On his hands the man in the chair wore leather gloves, and in one gloved hand he held a cigarette.

"Do you know who I am?" said a voice from the darkness; a voice that sounded strange to Maguire; gravelly, but with a curious rattling at the back of the throat.

"N-no..." Maguire stuttered. He could taste blood, like old coins.

"But you've heard of me," said the man in the pinstriped suit, lifting up his cigarette into the shadows. Floating in the darkness, the burning tip flared a brighter orange and then a billowing cloud of blue-grey smoke spilled out into the light.

"I... I don't know..." said Maguire, "I don't know who you are..." ▸

"IT'S NOT JUST ANY BOOK," SAID THE MAN IN THE SUIT, "IT'S THE BOOK OF JAHI. YOUR FRIEND FRANK WOULDN'T TELL US WHERE IT WAS, EITHER. WE HAD TO LET HIM GO."

"Oh, you've heard of me," said the man in the pinstripe suit.

"I swear," said Maguire, "I don't know what you're talking about."

Suddenly one of the two men with shaved heads lunged forward and delivered a punishing blow to Maguire's lower back. A bolt of pain shot through his body, as he swung back and forth on the hook.

"Tell me about the Book," said the man in the pinstriped suit.

"What book?" Maguire sobbed.

"The Book Of Jahi. Where is it?"

"I don't know about any book..."

Now the other skinhead stepped forward, slamming his fist into Maguire's stomach as if he were little more than a punchbag.

"It's not just *any* book," said the man in the pinstriped suit. "It's the Book Of Jahi. Your friend Frank wouldn't tell us where it was, either. We had to let him go."

Struggling to remain conscious, Maguire looked up at the figure half-hidden in the shadows. It was now that he became aware of two other people in the room, standing either side of the chair. Though he couldn't see their faces he saw that they too were wearing immaculately tailored suits.

"Who *are* you people?" he asked, barely able to form the words.

Still obscured by the darkness the three men laughed; a throaty, guttural cackling that terrified Maguire. The man in the pinstriped suit shifted in his chair. He flicked his cigarette to the ground and stubbed it out with his toe.

"You know who I am," he said, leaning forward, further into the light.

Only now could Maguire see his face. Only now could he see that this man, this *thing*, had slimy, amphibious skin patterned with jagged black and red stripes. Only now did he see that the top of his head was crested with a series of webbed spines, almost like a Mohawk made of semi-translucent flesh. Only now could he see the creature's shapeless mouth, its fleshy lips barely concealing rows of tiny jagged teeth.

The two men standing either side of him now stepped forward, both of them still laughing, and Maguire saw that they too were as monstrous as that thing in the chair. The head of the first was blue with misshapen yellow spots, while the second was streaked with dark purple and green.

"What *are* you?" screamed Maguire.

The creature in the pinstripe suit laughed.

"I'm Mr Glee..." he said, "and these are my associates, Mr Croker and Mr Lime. Boys... Take him away."

Maguire wriggled and fought, still dangling from the hook, but the monsters in suits were upon him before he could scream another word.

CONTINUED ON PAGE 30!

DID YOU KNOW CAPTAIN JACK CAN SNIFF PARTS OF HIMSELF NO HUMAN CAN? THAT'S JOHN BARROWMAN'S JACK RUSSELL, 'CAPTAIN JACK', OF COURSE! READ ON FOR MORE SUCH EXTRAORDINARY INSIGHTS!

What is the full name on your birth certificate?
"John Scot Barrowman. Scot with one T!"

What is your nickname?
"Jinny Bazza is the one that everyone knows. That's a name that was created by Eve Myles. I answer to that or 'J' most of the time."

What is your earliest memory?
"Riding my Big Wheel tricycle down our street in Mount Vernon in Glasgow, with everyone looking at me going, 'Oh my gosh! What is that?' We'd brought it back with us from America, and no one had ever seen one over here. It's just a plastic low-riding trike for kids, but it looks like a souped-up hotrod. It was awesome!"

When was your first kiss?
"My first, most important kiss was when I was 19 or 20. It was in a swimming pool in Nashville, Tennessee, with a guy I had fallen for, and it was under the stars in the middle of the night."

What was the last dream you had?
"This is terrible, but I was dreaming that Charlotte Church was getting really ticked off at me because I was flirting with [her partner] Gavin Henson! I was going to give him a great big snog, and she was saying, [adopts a strong Welsh accent] 'John Barrowman, if you touch him I'll kill you!' Let's just say I woke up very happy..."

When was the last time you cried?
"I cried with laughter yesterday. My partner Scott came back from an assault course saying he was in severe agony. I was on the telephone to my sister, and we were making fun of him, saying it was only because he'd been trying to impress another guy on the course. Turned out he was actually sick, and we had to rush him to hospital at 2am! He's fine now, but we were laughing so hard before we knew!"

Do you believe in aliens and the supernatural?
"I have to think there is life out there, even if it's not within our solar system, or even our galaxy. It would be a bit arrogant to think there wasn't anything else. As for the supernatural, yes I do believe, but for personal reasons that I don't like to talk about." ▶

JOHN BARROWMAN

What makes you happy?
"Lots of things make me happy, but one of the things that makes me happiest is the fact I'm doing what I love to do, and every day I get to go to work with a grin on my face!"

What really winds you up?
"Inconsistency and lying! I've got hundreds of examples of people doing that in my life. It really bugs me when people are asked to do something and they don't do it, and then they give you an excuse. Don't even bother! Be honest with me and say you didn't have the time, or you couldn't be arsed, but don't make up some kind of lie as to why you didn't do it. I also hate people chewing gum around me! They're like cows chewing cud!"

What are you scared of?
"I think everybody knows that I don't like to fly, because I really don't like turbulence. I'm not sure I'm afraid of it, though. There are not many things I'm afraid of. I'll try almost anything as long as I can assess the risk and make sure it doesn't put me in unnecessary danger. I try not to look at things from a fear point of view."

If you had a superpower what would it be?
"Funnily enough, given what I said about planes, I'd love to be able to fly. I would fly every day, just for the quiet and the calm. I'd be up in the air, and no one would be able to get in touch with me."

What is your most embarrassing memory?
"Crapping my pants on stage while I was dancing. I had diarrhoea and it ran down my white trousers until I started kicking it over the front row of the audience. I was in a show called I Hear America Singing Its Song and someone put a laxative in my water as a joke. When I was out on stage, I farted and immediately felt the warm sensation going all down my leg and start to seep through. If someone's got it on video, I want to see, because now I think it would be hysterical."

What's the worst thing you've ever done?
"When I was a kid, we used to get rolls of toilet paper and chuck them into the trees near people's homes. We'd drape the trees in something like 50 rolls of toilet paper, and then wait for it to rain, because when it gets wet, the toilet paper sticks into the trees and you can't get it out. I do not recommend people do it, though, because one time we got busted, and we had to clean it up. That is not a good job."

What is your most treasured possession?
"My dogs: Captain Jack, or CJ, who's a Jack Russell, and an English Cocker Spaniel named Charlie."

What is on your mp3 player?
"Oh, it's one of the most eclectic collections you could find! Anything from Barbara Streisand and the soundtrack to the musical Wicked, to Bon Jovi, Joni Mitchell and Maroon 5. There's something for everybody on my iPod!"

"I WISH PEOPLE WOULD STOP ASKING ME HOW IT FEELS TO LOOK LIKE TOM CRUISE!"

What single item would you want with you on a desert island?
"It would be a combination of two things, if that's allowed. I'd have a television and Sky Plus! At the very least, it would have to be a TV with digital built in, so I had the choice of channels."

What are you drinking?
"My drink of choice would be a double Gray Goose vodka and tonic."

Can you tell us a joke?
"I have a brilliantly rude joke that you can't print, which is terrible, because I've been dying to tell someone! Here's one that's not rude: a one-armed man is hanging from a tree. How do you get him down? Wave to him!"

What question do you wish you were asked in interviews?
"I get asked every question. I wish people would stop asking me how it feels to look kind of like Tom Cruise! When people ask me that I think, 'You idiot!' I really can't think of anything I would particularly want to be asked, though."

What is the strangest place you have ever seen your image?
"Well, we ran a contest on my official website (www.johnbarrowman.com) where people sent in photos of me in interesting places, so there have been a few! They either created them digitally, or took a picture of me with them wherever they went! But one woman got in trouble because she put pictures of me up all over an art gallery in Wisconsin. She just started putting them on the walls next to paintings!"

THE FASHION HUB

SAVING THE WORLD IN STYLE IS ALWAYS TOP PRIORITY FOR TORCHWOOD COSTUME DESIGNER **RAY HOLMAN**. WE ASKED HIM WHAT THE HOTTEST HEROES ARE WEARING THIS SEASON.

JACK WEARS

▶ MATINEE IDOL

"We always wanted to keep the World War Two hero look for Captain Jack, so all his outfits have a 1940s flavour. We knew he'd be running around an awful lot, so I redesigned his RAF Group Captain's greatcoat from Doctor Who to make it more fluid, because the real things are very weighty. John is allergic to wool, so we used a cotton moleskin instead, which is much lighter and gives you that movement and flowing silhouette.

"JACK HAS SPEAR-POINT COLLARS AND DOUBLE CUFFS."

"The rest of Jack's costumes are loosely wartime based, so he has big, period trousers, which are getting more and more styled to suit his figure, and shirts from a shirt-maker with spear-point collars and double cuffs. He also has some lovely silver cufflinks that are shaped like Spitfires! Unlike the rest of the team, all John's clothes are made from scratch.

"There are actually five Captain Jack coats in use on the show: one 'hero' version, which is used for most scenes; one 'wet' coat made with a pre-shrunk fabric; a 'running' coat that is slightly shorter so John's heels don't catch when he runs; and two stunt coats, which were hero coats back in series one."

IANTO WEARS:

▶ CITY SLICKER

"Ianto has a very distinct look, but his suits actually vary quite a lot. He started off with some nice-but-boring Marks and Spencer's suits in series one, which were top-end, fitted ones, but always very sober. Towards the end of series one, I'd also got him into a waistcoat, and everyone thought that looked really good.

"For series two, we evolved the look quite a lot, and now his suits come from all over the place. It's just a question of where

"IANTO'S EVOLVING INTO SOMETHING MUCH SHARPER."

I see something that looks right for Gareth, so I've bought him a suit from Savile Row and suits from Zara and Next.

"We also realised we could be a bit more flash with Ianto, now he's come out of the background and started to assert himself a bit more. So we moved him onto coloured shirts and snazzier ties, which add a nice, lively touch, and we continued to mix it up a bit with the waistcoats as well. He started off in fairly butlerish white and grey shirts, but we realised his skin tones can take the extra colour, and now he's evolving into something much sharper, which looks really good filmed in High Definition."

GWEN WEARS:

▶ BIKER GROOVER

"Gwen's look has changed quite a lot across the series, because she wasn't wearing leather when she was just out of the police force. She started off in series one with a kind of faded, high street look, wearing things like Miss Sixty jeans, but she's become quite a lot more designer and heroic-looking as her confidence has grown and she's become more established as a part of Torchwood.

"For series two, we found her some better jeans from America, which are

"GWEN WORE A LOT MORE LEATHER IN SERIES TWO."

made by a company called 7 For All Mankind, and we started to put her in leather a lot more. She wears leading brands like Diesel and G-Star now, and Belstaff, which specialises in bikers' leathers. It's a sexy look, but it's also quite practical.

"As with all the main characters, Gwen's leathers toughen her up a bit, but keep her stylish at the same time. They all have to run around and fight aliens and do stunts and things, so they can't be in soft fabrics or anything that's not hard-wearing. For the same reason, Gwen will always wear flat-soled Converse or Belstaff boots, and we only put her into heels when she was getting married."

LLEOLIAD LLEOLIAD LLEOLIAD!

THAT'S **LOCATION, LOCATION, LOCATION** TO ANY NON-WELSH SPEAKERS, AND THAT'S WHAT THE NEXT 10 PAGES ARE ALL ABOUT! SO WHY NOT TAKE A TOUR AROUND SOME OF THE SHOW'S REAL WORLD SETTINGS?

BLOWFISH. SPACE WHALES. SHAPESHIFTERS. Time Agents. They've all travelled across the galaxy just to spend a little quality time in Cardiff. And why not, with its lively community and vibrant cultural life? There's plenty to see and do further afield in South Wales, too, with beautiful countryside and rich history never far away.

But in recent years, a new wave of visitors has been heading for this part of the world, in search of the sites and sights that give Torchwood its distinctly local look. These locations may crop up regularly in Doctor Who, but they are disguised and dressed as many different times and places. It is Torchwood that really puts Wales on the television map.

So this issue, we thought we'd do something similar and put Torchwood on the map – literally. Over the next eight pages, we've selected some choice Torchwood locations from series one and two and pinpointed them for your visiting pleasure. In the city centre and the Bay, we've even suggested possible walking routes for a sunny day out or two on a Torchwood tour!

We hope our maps will be useful to you, but we recommend you use them in conjunction with an Ordnance Survey map (particularly if venturing further out into the wilds of Wales), and always plan your journey in advance if using public transport! We've tried to include all the major locations here, but have for the most part left out private residences. The information has been compiled from production callsheets and with help from fan website www.torchwoodlocations.com Be sure to check out the site for even more location information! Eve Myles is said to be a fan... ▶

CITY WALK

BAY WALK

4 **HIGH STREET ARCADE AND CASTLE ARCADE** From Cathays Park, head back towards the High Street, where two of the Victorian arcades have particular interest for Torchwood fans. The High Street Arcade is home to the roller shutter that Gwen slides under, Indiana Jones-style in Ghost Machine, while Castle Arcade is the location of Bilis Manger's shop, A Stitch In Time, in End Of Days.

3 **CITY HALL AND NATIONAL MUSEUM** Leave the riverside to take a walk through Bute Park to Cathays Park, where the impressive City Hall forms the centrepiece of this Edwardian civic centre. The 60-metre high clock tower is where Jack looks out over the city in Greeks Bearing Gifts, while the nearby National Museum serves as Aberystwyth's Science and Natural History Museum in Random Shoes.

2 **MILLENNIUM STADIUM** Head towards the imposing Millennium Stadium until you reach the River Taff. This is one of the places where Tosh hears people's thoughts in Greeks Bearing Gifts, and the embankment on the opposite side is where the team walk and talk in Ghost Machine. In Out of Time, John Ellis is dropped off at gate three, on the other side of the stadium.

1 **CARDIFF CENTRAL TRAIN AND BUS STATION** Whether you're road-tripping to Cardiff or braving public transport, make your first port of call Cardiff's main railway station. In Ghost Machine, Gwen runs through the front entrance of the station while chasing Bernie, before shifting back in time to World War Two. Adjacent to the station is the city's central bus station, where Emma leaves Gwen to take a coach to London in Out Of Time. From here, you can catch buses to most Cardiff locations.

9 **CHIPPY LANE** A right turn on to Hayes Bridge Road followed by a left leads onto Caroline Street. Known locally as Chippy Lane, the route is full of takeaways, but in Day One, it is awash with images of sex as Carys passes by.

10 **CARDIFF MARKET** Caroline Street leads onto St Mary St, home to the indoor market where Mark chokes on rose petals in Small Worlds. From here, the railway station is just a short walk away, for rail and bus services to the Bay (see below) or locations further afield (see over the page)!

SERIES ONE CARDIFF

100 metres

2 **COAL EXCHANGE** Cross Lloyd George Avenue and head along James Street to reach the Coal Exchange in Mount Stuart Square. Currently closed for refurbishment, this is where the organised Weevil fight took place in Combat.

3 **ST DAVID'S HOTEL** A room in this classy waterfront venue served as Owen's flat in Countrycide. Take in the impressive exterior and views across the Bay, or book a room for an extended stay! Toshiko's more modest flat, seen in Greeks Bearing Gifts, is on the nearby Windsor Esplanade.

5 QUEEN STREET

A trip to Cardiff wouldn't be complete without a walk down Queen Street – the city's busiest shopping area. Here, you'll be following in the footsteps of Gwen and Owen, who run this way in Ghost Machine, Tosh, who stands outside the Queen's Arcade when she first listens to the thoughts of the public around her in Greeks Bearing Gifts, and Abaddon, who towers over the street in End Of Days.

6 WINDSOR PLACE

Off the far end of Queen Street, this road is home to the fertility clinic where Carys works in Day One, and Buffalo Bar, where Jack takes Gwen in Everything Changes.

7 CINEWORLD

From Windsor Place, head back onto Queen Street, then take a left down Churchill Way, turning right onto Bridge Street, then left again onto Mary Ann Street. Here you will pass the Cineworld cinema and the former site of the NCP car park where Gwen first spied the Torchwood team, in the alleyway between the two buildings, in Everything Changes. Gwen and PC Andy return to the car park later in the episode.

8 ALTOLUSSO BUILDING

From Cineworld, head along Bute Terrace, passing the ultra-modern Altolusso apartment complex on your left, where Captain Jack keeps watch on the city in the sweeping aerial shot first seen in Everything Changes.

1 HOLLYWOOD BOWL

Part of the Bay's Red Dragon Centre, this bowling alley is where Gwen and Rhys shared a date in Day One. Cardiff's very own Doctor Who exhibition is also located here, making it an ideal place to start or finish a tour of this area.

ALL HAIL THE GREAT DEVOURER, COME TO FEAST ON LIFE!

PLACES TO EAT AND DRINK FROM SERIES ONE

FOOD

A RAMON'S This Salisbury Road institution serves Gwen two eggs, ham and chips in Random Shoes.

B LA TASCA Gwen and Linda go to this restaurant in the Brewery Quarter on St Mary's Road in Random Shoes.

C ASK Gwen and Rhys' date at this Mill Lane restaurant is interrupted by the blazing meteor in Day One.

D MUMBAI BAY This Indian takeaway in James Street became Jubilee Pizza in Everything Changes.

E THE PEARL OF THE ORIENT Owen and Diane go to this Mermaid Quay venue in Out of Time.

DRINK

F TIGER TIGER In Combat, Owen goes to this bar on Greyfriars Road for a drink and ends up in a fight.

G THE FAT CAT CAFÉ BAR In Greeks Bearing Gifts, this Greyfriars Road bar is where Tosh meets Mary.

H BUFFALO BAR Located on Windsor Place, this is where Jack retcons Gwen in Everything Changes.

I MINKSYS SHOW BAR This cabaret venue in cathedral Walk is where the alien gas strikes in Day One.

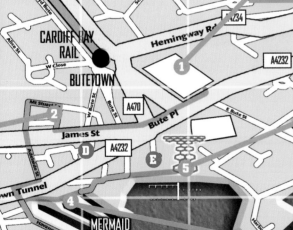

5 ROALD DAHL PLASS

No trip to Torchwood's Cardiff would be complete without visiting Roald Dahl Plass, the home of the Hub itself! Here you can find the iconic water tower that houses Torchwood's Rift manipulator technology, as well as the paving slab that allows the team access to their base. The Millennium Centre can also be found here, and just around the corner, right on the waterfront, is the 'Tourist Information' back door to the Hub, seen in various episodes. If you make it this far on your tour, be sure to send us a photo of yourself at the Bay!

4 MERMAID QUAY

Cyberwoman's claustrophobic feel was achieved by filming mostly in the Hub, but one scene was filmed opposite Mermaid Quay, when Rhys phoned Gwen near the end of the episode.

TOWN HALL, MERTHYR TYDFIL
Used for the exterior of The Ritz in Captain Jack Harkness, Merthyr's old town hall can be found on the High Street, though the side of the building seen in the episode is actually on Newcastle Street. The interiors were filmed in Newport (see facing page).

PENWYLLT This village about 40 miles outside of Cardiff was the main location for Countrycide, with the surrounding area also featured heavily.

GLYNTAFF CEMETERY, PONTYPRIDD Known locally as Ponty, this is the birthplace of Tom Jones and final resting place of Eugene Jones in Random Shoes. It is 12 miles north of Cardiff.

RADYR PRIMARY SCHOOL, RADYR
In Small Worlds, Jasmine attends this school, renamed Coed y Carreg primary on screen. An outer suburb of Cardiff, Radyr is about five miles north-west of the city centre.

THE CORNWALL, GRANGETOWN
West of the city centre, in the Grangetown suburb of Cardiff, this pub in Cornwall Street is where Gwen and PC Andy attend a brawl in Everything Changes.

MOD ST ATHAN Formerly RAF St Athan, this Ministry of Defence base near the village of the same name in the Vale of Glamorgan is not open to the public, but features prominently in Out Of Time.

BARRY SHOOTING RANGE, BARRY ISLAND The interior of this Hub lookalike location, about seven miles south-west of Cardiff, is where Jack teaches Gwen to shoot in Ghost Machine.

CRICKHOWELL

ABERGAVENNY

ABERCYNON SERVICES, A470 This service area on the northbound side of the A470, north of Pontypridd, is where Eugene arranges to meet the mysterious buyer of his Dogon Sixth Eye in Random Shoes.

WESTGATE HOTEL, NEWPORT Sadly, the opulent Westgate is no longer a working hotel, but its impressive reception, bar and ballroom were used for the interior of The Ritz in Captain Jack Harkness. The building is located at the Bridge Street end of Stow Hill in Newport, and was the site of the 1839 Chartist uprising. Bullet holes can still be seen in the door frame!

5 kilometres

A48

CASTELL COCH, TONGWYNLAIS This 19th Century castle has yet to feature prominently in Torchwood (despite doubling for a German *schloss* in the Doctor Who series four finale, Journey's End), but the forest behind the castle was used as the landing site of the meteor in Day One. The castle is off exit 32 of the M4, and a footpath runs through the woods.

NEWPORT

A48

CARDIFF

PAGET ROOMS AND ARCHER ROAD BRIDGE, PENARTH The Paget Rooms in Station Road, Penarth, are the venue for Estelle's talk on fairies in Small Worlds, while Jasmine walks home along the nearby footpath that runs parallel, along the disused railway and under Archer Road. Penarth is located just across the Bay, four miles from Cardiff city centre.

PENARTH

BARRY DOCKS Seven miles south-west of Cardiff, Barry docks serve as Hedley Quay in They Keep Killing Suzie. According to Toshiko's map in the episode, the fictional quay is in the north-west of the country.

8 GLAMORGAN BUILDING
Head back towards the city centre via Cathays Park, where this grand civic building, now part of Cardiff University, interiors of were used for Parker's mansion in A Day In The Death.

9 BUTE PARK
Cross over North Road into Bute Park, where Owen is briefly seen running in A Day In The Death. The park was also used for the circus scenes in From Out Of The Rain.

10 CARDIFF CASTLE
Why not finish this walk with a trip round Cardiff Castle? This is where Captain John takes Jack before setting off his city-wide bombs in Exit Wounds.

4 WHARTON STREET
Turn right off Westgate Street and cross over St Mary's Road to reach Wharton Street, which runs along the side of department store Howells. This is where Owen stands as life passes him by in A Day In The Death.

3 COUNTY COURT BUILDING
At the other end of Park Street to the stadium, turn left onto Westgate Street, where a member of Cell 114 blows up the telecommunications headquarters – actually a disused county court building – in Sleeper.

2 STADIUM HOUSE
Cross over Wood Street and head for the stadium. On Park Street is Wales' tallest building, Stadium House, used as the exterior of the Central Server Building where Tosh and Ianto encounter the cowled figures at the start of Exit Wounds.

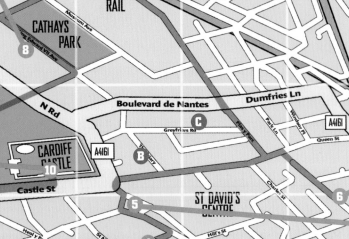

1 NCP CAR PARK
Near the train station on Wood Street and Great Western Lane, the roof of this car park appears at the beginning and end of Kiss Kiss, Bang Bang as the site of Captain John's personal Rift storm. From here, John hurls a mugger to his death and nearly blows the team up with a bomb DNA-locked to his chest. The car park shows up again in Dead Man Walking, when Weevils pusue Jack and Owen in order to worship the recently deceased Owen.

SERIES TWO CARDIFF

1 CANAL PARK
You can walk between the city centre and the Bay (or take a bus) down the long Lloyd George Avenue, but why not go down Canal parade, south of St Mary's Street, and wander the length of Canal Park down to Stuart Street in the Bay? As the name and shape of the park suggest, this was once a canal, but its Torchwood significance is as the site of Jack and Adam's nighttime talk in Adam, roughly level with Hannah Street and Alice Street.

2 STUART STREET
This is where one of the alien sleeper agents activates, abandoning her baby in Sleeper.

100 metres

CITY WALK BAY WALK

7 TOWER BUILDING Another high-rise location can be found by retracing your steps along Churchill Way, then along Park Place to the appropriately named Tower Building, which houses Cardiff University's School of Psychology, where Owen meets Maggie in A Day In The Death.

6 HELMONT HOUSE Right turns onto Queen Street and then onto Churchill Way will bring you to this British Gas building, where Captain John pushes Jack to his death in Kiss Kiss, Bang Bang. Appreciate it from the pavement below, where Jack was left splayed across a bench.

5 ST JOHN'S CHURCH Wharton Street leads into The Hayes and Trinity Street, where Gwen pursues the male Nostrovite in Something Borrowed. Turn left towards St John's Church, where Jack eventually kills the shapeshifter.

3 ROALD DAHL PLASS The home of the Hub is where the team says goodbye to Martha in A Day In The Death. Walk further down towards the 'tourist information' facade to see where Ianto presents Jack with coffee in Fragments.

4 JETTY Owen jumps into the Bay from here in A Day in the Death, but we recommend you simply admire the view!

I SHALL WALK THE EARTH AND MY HUNGER WILL KNOW NO BOUNDS!
PLACES TO EAT AND DRINK FROM SERIES TWO

FOOD

A MIMOSA This restaurant in Mermaid Quay can be seen behind the alien paramedic in Sleeper.

DRINK

B STEAM BAR Owen heads for this bar in The Friary (part of the Hilton Hotel) in Dead Man Walking.

C TIGER TIGER This Greyfriars Road venue hosts Jack and John's violent reunion in Kiss Kiss, Bang Bang.

D THE ELI JENKINS Tosh and Tommy drink and play pool in this Bute Crescent pub in To The Last Man.

E THE WATERGUARD This futuristic looking building on Harbour Drive is young Jack's home in Adam.

5 WELSH ASSEMBLY BUILDING Just behind the redbrick Pierhead building, the Assembly steps are where Rhys and Gwen eat ice creams at the end of Meat.

6 NORWEGIAN CHURCH Tosh and Tommy admire the statue of Captain Scott alongside the Norwegian Church on Harbour Drive in To The Last Man. The church is now an arts centre.

ALEXANDRA DOCK

BRECON BEACONS
ATIONAL PARK

MARGAM COUNTRY PARK The Orangery on this large estate is where Gwen and Rhys exchanged vows in Something Borrowed. The exterior scenes were shot in Dyffrym Gardens in the Vale of Glamorgan (see below), but Margam is about three miles east of Port Talbot.

PHOENIX CINEMA, TON PENTRE This working cinema in the Rhondda Valley is where the Electro interiors were captured in From Out Of The Rain. The exterior can be found on the other side of Cardiff, in Penarth (see facing page).

ST MATTHEW'S CHURCH, PONTYPRIDD This deconsecrated church in Dorothy Street became St Mary's at the start of Dead Man Walking. About 12 miles north of Cardiff, it is now being converted into flats – hopefully Weevil-free!

A404

ME
T

A4054

A472

DDA

PONTYPRIDD

MAESTEG

YNYSANGHARAD PARK LIDO This disused swimming pool is no longer open to the public, and has long since fallen into disrepair. A registered charity is currently campaigning for refurbishment of the site, where the Ghost Maker and Pearl took refuge in From Out Of The Rain.

A4119

CAERPHI

ABERKENFIG

MERTHYR ROAD, WHITCHURCH The very first location of series two, this outer suburb of Cardiff is where the team chase the Blowfish in Kiss Kiss, Bang Bang.

BRIDG

GLANRHYD HOSPITAL, BRIDGEND Used for both the 1918 and present day sequences, this hospital became St Teilo's in To The Last Man, located about 16 miles west of Cardiff.

A4232

A48

DINAS POWYS

PORT

BARRY

MERTHYR MAWR SAND DUNES These dunes have a Hollywood history as the location for David Lean's Lawrence of Arabia, but they also doubled as Jack's childhood home, the Boeshane Peninsula, in Adam.

DYFFRYN GARDENS These botanical gardens near the village of St Nicholas in the Vale of Glamorgan provided the exteriors for Gwen and Rhys's wedding day in Something Borrowed, with interiors shot at Margam Country Park (see above). The gardens are open to the public, and are currently being restored to their former glory.

CRICKHOWELL

AB

RYNMAWR

A4046

CAERWENT MILITARY TRAINING AREA, CALDICOT A regular haunt of the Torchwood production team, this military base is not open to the public, but serves as Jonah's care home in Adrift, the booby-trapped building in Fragments, and, less surprisingly, the army base in Sleeper.

SERIES TWO SOUTH WALES

29

5 kilometres

ST CADOC'S HOSPITAL, CAERLEON The red-brick exterior seen as Jack and Gwen drive away from 'City Cardiff Hospital' in Sleeper, is in fact St Cadoc's in Caerlon, Newport, about 12 miles from Cardiff.

A

P0

A4046

A

44

A48

A4048

A468

STRAD YNACH

CARDIFF BARRAGE This feat of modern engineering stretches across the Bay and links Cardiff to Penarth by means of a new pedestrian walkway. In Adrift, the young Jonah is seen walking home along the route.

CARDIFF UNIVERSITY The Optometry and Visual Sciences building here is where Owen wrestles with Death at the climax of Dead Man Walking.

NEWPORT

PAGET ROOMS AND WINDSOR TEA ROOMS, PENARTH Also seen in series one's Small Worlds, the Paget Rooms in Station Road, Penarth, serves as the exterior of the Electro cinema in From Out Of The Rain. Nearby, in Windor Road, the Windsor Tea Rooms are where the Ghost Maker and Pearl take their second victim, as she closes up her cafe for the night.

CARDIFF

PENARTH

FLAT HOLM Though named as the location of Jonah's care home in Adrift, only the exterior shots were actually filmed on Flat Holm island, five miles offshore of Cardiff. The island is a nature reserve and a Site of Special Scientific Interest. Trips to the island can be booked between March and October.

PENARTH PIER, PENARTH Tosh and Tommy share a romantic moment on this late Victorian pier in To The Last Man, just across the Bay, five miles from Cardiff.

IANTO LOOKED DOWN AT THE GRAFFITI ON THE SIDE OF THE SUV and shook his head. "Hardly Banksy, is it?" he said. "I suppose I'll be the one buying the paint, then?"

"If you could," said Jack, patting him on the shoulder. "I believe the correct colour is called Obsidian Night."

"Oh, I like that," said Ianto. "Obsidian Night. Sounds like a '70s rock group." Jack laughed softly, but Gwen didn't share his amusement.

"How's Kelly?" she asked. She was talking about Kelly Jenkins, the pretty, ʒde young woman who had been a widow no more than four hours. Kelly ʒns who, for the last few weeks at least, had lived inside the weathered and ʒlooking caravan outside which Jack, Gwen and Ianto now stood.

"She's at the safe house," said Ianto, "The nice one, in Llandaff. Said she ʒed to be left alone for a bit. Which I suppose is fair enough, given what ʒ been through today."

"Yes," said Jack, "it is. How are Fred and Ginger doing?"

ʒnto frowned.

"ʒosh and Owen," said Jack, smiling. "Any clues?"

ʒnto nodded.

"You could say that," he said. "One pretty big clue, I'd say."

ʒe gestured with a nod toward the entrance of the caravan, and together ʒ walked in.

ʒespite the best efforts of Owen and Toshiko the caravan still looked very ʒ like a murder scene. It still smelled of death, and death's presence could ʒe felt; that unmistakable chill and a souring of the air with which they ʒ all so familiar; none more so than Owen.

"ʒhat have you got for us?" asked Jack, looking at each of them in turn. ʒko held up the plastic DVD case with its simple message visible through ʒuter cover:

ʒR TORCHWOOD.

ʒck looked from the plastic case to Toshiko and back again.

"Have you watched it?" he asked.

"ʒ little," said Toshiko. "It's very... Illuminating. But it seems we might have ʒbled into something big."

"Well, put it on!" said Jack, enthusiastically.

ʒoshiko nodded and loaded the disc into the dead man's DVD player. ʒ only when she turned on the television that they all noticed the ʒon smear of blood across the screen.

"Oh," said Owen, stepping forward with a cloth, "looks like I missed a bit." ʒe mopped at the screen until it was clear, and they gathered around, ʒng down at the television. Seconds later, the image appeared of ʒddle-aged man with silvery greying hair and tanned skin. It was Frank ʒns, the man whose death had brought them here in the first place.

"Hello," he said, smiling at the camera. "If you're watching this, that ʒs I'm probably dead. Feels funny saying that. Like one of those things ʒle only ever say in films. Now, the only one of you whose name ʒw is Jack Harkness, and I'm guessing you know who I am.

"ʒf I am dead, then the reason is the Book of Jahi. The first thing you ʒld probably know is that it's not a book. Not really. That's just its name. ʒore like a key, really... Except it doesn't look like a key, either. "

"Okay," said Owen, "now I'm really confused..."

"ʒ know, I know," said Frank Jenkins. "It's all a bit confusing."

"Well that's just plain creepy," said Owen.

"ʒnyway," Frank continued, "there's a character you might ʒ heard of called Mr Glee, and he wants that Book more ʒ anything that's ever come through the Rift.

"ʒhe thing is... The Book can be used to open up ʒtorms, any time, any place. It's like the ultimate ʒton key. Mr Glee is a thief. He's a gangster.

He's a lot more besides, believe me. The Book could come in very handy to a man, well, not a *man*... It could come in very handy to *someone* like that.

"The problem is, and I'm sure you lot already know this, messing about with Rift storms is dangerous. It's not the kind of power you want ending up in the hands of someone like Mr Glee.

"That's why I never sold it on. I've sold powerful things to bad people in the past, and made a very nice living out of it, but not this time. All things considered, I thought it probably for the best that the Book was destroyed, but if I'm dead, and you're watching this, then that means there's a chance it won't be.

"The Book is hidden in our flat, up in Cwmblaidd. I buried it under the floorboards in the living room before we left. Believe me, I tried destroying it about a dozen other ways, but nothing made a dent. In the end, I thought it best to just leave it there. Depending on when you're watching this, it might be under about a million gallons of water, which is the best place for it.

"If it's *not*, then you guys might just have a chance to get to it first. And if you *do*... Well, there's a few things you need to know about the Book."

THE BOOK OF

Frank leaned forward and turned the camera slightly, so that its aim was now fixed on a large pad of white paper, on which he'd drawn a rectangular object covered with small buttons and dials.

"This is what it looks like," he said, pointing at the drawing. "Now, the part here..."

"Ah," said Jack, "the science bit. Tosh: that's your department. Take the disc back to the Hub and find out what you can about that Book. Ianto: I need you to head back to the Hub and cross-reference any files we might have on this Mr Glee. Owen: get to the safe house and make sure Kelly's okay."

Owen grimaced.

"Why me? Gwen's much better doing at the whole shoulder-to-cry-on bit."

"Because she might still be in shock," said Jack. "And I want Gwen to call on her cute little policeman friend and ask him what he knows about Mr Glee. Then we'll all meet back at the Hub in three hours."

"And then what do we do?" said Gwen. "About the book, I mean?"

"Then," said Jack, "we go find it."

By the time Gwen got to the central police station in Cathays Park, the sun was shining and the last puddles beginning to dry out. The morning's rainstorms were all but forgotten.

Her one-time colleague, PC Andy, was waiting for her on the steps, fresh out of uniform at the end of his shift.

"So," he said, "I suppose it's too much to hope you're after a garden variety burglar or car thief? What is it this time? Death Star over Ponty?"

"Mr Glee," said Gwen.

"Oh," said Andy, his smile fading. "*Him*. Come on, then. Let's walk."

They began strolling along the wide boulevard between the gleaming Portland stone edifices of the civic centre.

"Now, Mr Glee is an interesting character," Andy began.

"What do you know about him?" Gwen chipped in, impatiently.

"Well, nothing really," Andy said. "There's literally nothing to know. He's a man of mystery. A bit like Kevin Spacey in The Usual Suspects."

"I haven't seen it."

"Oh," said Andy. "Forget I said anything, then. Wouldn't want to spoil the twist. But Mr Glee? We've had people mentioning him for years. Remember that big bank robbery last year?"

"Not really, no," said Gwen.

"Well," Andy continued, "one of the guys we arrested for that said the mastermind was Mr Glee. Of course, he'd never met Mr Glee, never even seen him. Then ▶

JAHI PART 2
BY DAVID LLEWELLYN
ILLUSTRATIONS MIKE DOWLING

there was that shooting in Fairwater. And when they found that body in a shopping bag – well, shopping bags? Everyone said it was Mr Glee, but when we tried tracing it back: nothing. Just like that," Andy blew a kiss on the air, "he's gone."

Gwen stopped walking.

"So you think he's made up?"

"Well," said Andy, "that's the thing. I wouldn't say he *doesn't* exist. But then, I've no proof to say he does."

"So what are the police doing about him?"

Andy laughed softly.

"We've got a file on him as thick as a brick, but no leads. To be honest, it's all a bit embarrassing. If you believe the word on the street, Mr Glee practically runs this city, but nobody knows who he is, where he's from, or what he looks like. Although... There is one person who says they've seen him."

Gwen stopped walking.

"Really?"

"Yeah. Taye Shapiro. Former crook and all-round bad guy."

"And he says he's met Mr Glee?"

Andy nodded.

"Then I need to speak to him," said Gwen.

"Okay," said Andy, hesitantly. "If you insist."

Owen found it hard to believe they could think of this as the "nice" safe house. It wasn't that the place was particularly horrible: there was no mildew in the corners or cracks in the windows. It was a perfectly functioning house, overlooking the rolling fields of Bute Park and, in the distance, the city itself. But it was just so empty and soulless.

It had been so long since Torchwood last used the place. There was a fine layer of dust on the nearly empty bookshelves and the old television set that sat in one corner of the living room. The few books on the shelves included a dog-eared copy of Jaws and a school Bible from the 1950s, while below the television there sat an ancient VHS video player and a small collection of old films. Owen knew the air was stale and musty, though he no longer had a sense of smell.

Kelly was sat on the sofa, staring at the blank and silent television, a handkerchief balled up in her fist. Owen knocked at the open door gently, and she looked up at him, her eyes still red from crying.

"I just came by to see how you are," said Owen, awkwardly.

Kelly nodded, then returned her gaze to the dead television with a sigh.

"I just don't get it," she said, sobbing gently. "Why Frank? What did he ever do to anyone?"

Owen crossed the room and sat down in a facing armchair.

"That's what we're trying to find out," he said.

Kelly looked at him, scowling.

"And who are you, exactly?" she snapped. "You're obviously not the police."

"We're Torchwood..." Owen began, but Kelly cut him off.

"Yeah, that's what your friend said. The girl I spoke to earlier. But what's Torchwood? And where are the police? I mean. if somebody did... did *that* to Frank, then why aren't the police involved?"

"It's a bit complicated," said Owen.

"Complicated?" said Kelly, choking as she raised her voice. "What's that supposed to mean? How am I supposed to know that I can trust you?"

Owen hated this. Why couldn't Jack have sent Gwen? Gwen would cope with this better than he could. Patients were fine, and the families of patients he could deal with, but this was something else.

"Kelly," he said eventually. "Do you know what Frank was involved in? Do you know what he did for a living?"

Kelly sniffed, wiping her nose with the handkerchief, and shook her head.

"He sold antiques," she replied. "That's all he did. What do you mean, *'involved in'*?"

Owen paused and thought hard about what he was about to say. If Jack had been there he'd no doubt have found some diplomatic way to dodge the question, but Jack wasn't there. It was his call.

"Kelly..." he sighed. "Frank didn't sell antiques."

Kelly frowned at him.

"What do you mean?"

"He didn't sell antiques. He sold artefacts. Alien artefacts."

Kelly laughed desperately, shaking her head in disbelief.

"No," she said. "I don't know what kind of mind games you people are trying to play, but no. No... That's quite enough. I think I'd prefer it if you just left, thank you..."

"It's true," said Owen. "You see, and this is gonna sound nuts, but Cardiff's not like other cities. There's this thing – this Rift – and it's a bit like a doorway,

or a window. When it's open, things come through it. All kinds of things. Frank used to collect those things, and he sold them on to the highest bidder."

Kelly covered her eyes with her hands, still shaking her head.

"This is a dream," she said. "This is a dream. This is a dream. Any minute now I'm gonna wake up..."

"It's not," said Owen. "I know it sounds... Well, I know how it sounds. But it's true. That's who we are. Torchwood. We keep an eye on the Rift and make sure anything that comes through doesn't do too much damage. We're a bit like nightclub bouncers, I suppose. Well, not really. But that's why the police aren't involved."

Kelly fixed her gaze on him once more.

"Alien artefacts?" she repeated, sarcastically.

"Yes," said Owen.

"Okay, then," said Kelly. "But that doesn't explain why this happened, does it?"

"Frank had something they wanted."

"They? Who are they?"

"The people who killed him. They wanted an artefact. It's called the Book of Jahi."

"They killed him over a *book*?"

"It's not just a book. Frank said he buried it under the floorboards of your old flat. He said that it's still in Cwmblaidd."

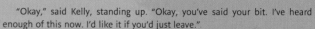

"Okay," said Kelly, standing up. "Okay, you've said your bit. I've heard enough of this now. I'd like it if you'd just leave."

Owen nodded, and got up to leave the room.

"Everything I've said is true," he said. "If you need anything, just call us."

"Go," said Kelly. "Please, just go."

Kelly walked him to the front door and saw him out into the street. Before Owen could say anything more, she had slammed the door shut in his face.

Returning to the living room and sitting back on the sofa, Kelly took a deep breath, sighed, and then flipped open her mobile phone. She punched in a number, lifted the phone to her ear and waited.

"It's me," she said, eventually. "I know where the Book is... Never mind that. Just send someone here to pick me up. You can take care of the girl. She's the one who'll know how to use it."

In the Hub, Ianto waited impatiently for Jack's call, but it didn't come. They had left him at Sunny Bay Caravan Park at his insistence. Though Ianto had said nothing, he could sense that Jack had been affected quite deeply by Frank Jenkins' message from beyond the grave. Maybe it was the fact that Frank had known his name. Whatever it was, Jack had stayed behind to finish the job of cleaning up, while Ianto and Tosh returned to the Hub.

After pouring himself another cup of coffee, and taking a bite from one of the doughnuts he had bought at Sunny Bay, Ianto returned to his computer.

"Found anything interesting?" Toshiko called over from her desk.

"Mm," said Ianto, with his mouth still full, "I think so."

Toshiko stood up and crossed the Hub, crouching down beside him and peering at his screen.

"What's that?" she asked, squinting at a black and white microfiche of a newspaper cutting.

"An old story from The Western Mail," said Ianto, then, reading from the microfiche, "Bute Town boarding house investigated by police."

"When was this?" said Toshiko.

"May, 1929."

"And what's it got to do with the Book? Or Mr Glee?"

"Look here," said Ianto, pointing at the screen. "Police investigating allegations of sordid and immoral activities at a Seager Street boarding house are now searching for the property's elusive owner, a character known only as Mr Glee."

Toshiko shrugged.

"Yeah," she said. "Maybe. I should go and get that book."

"Good thinking."

"If Jack comes back tell him... I don't know... Tell him I had to buy 'women's things'. That usually works with men."

Ianto laughed as Toshiko turned, walking quickly towards the exit.

"Be quick!" he called out after her.

Gwen hated hospitals. She hated their sterility, and that disinfectant smell. She hated seeing the expressions of those visiting, whether they were gaunt and drained, or trying their best to be upbeat. It seemed even sadder, somehow, when the visitors were putting on a brave face.

The psychiatric unit at St Helen's was a different kind of hospital to the ones that Gwen was used to. There were fewer visitors, for one thing, and then there was the noise. From behind closed doors she heard every kind of sound a human being could make. She heard laughter and screaming, crying and shouting.

The doctor who had greeted them in the reception walked Gwen and Andy down an impossibly long corridor until they came to the incongruously cheerful-sounding day room, and pointed them in the direction of a young man seated in the far corner.

"Don't worry," said the doctor. "He won't bite. He's had his afternoon cocktail of happy pills."

Gwen nodded in silence, and together she and Andy crossed the room.

KELLY COVERED HER EYES WITH HER HANDS, STILL SHAKING HER HEAD. "THIS IS A DREAM," SHE SAID. "THIS IS A DREAM. THIS IS A DREAM. ANY MINUTE NOW, I'M GONNA WAKE UP..."

"You don't think...?"

"Well, you and Jack have been to a 1940s disco, and I seem to recall you dated a guy from 1918, so it's not exactly beyond the realms of possibility now, is it?"

"I suppose not," said Toshiko with a smile.

"How about you?" Ianto asked, "Has Frank given you any insight into that Book of his?"

"I'm not sure," Toshiko replied, turning and walking back to her work-station. Ianto followed her and saw on her monitor a freeze-frame of Frank Jenkins' drawing of the Book. Next to the drawing, Frank had written down a series of obscure symbols.

"What are they?" asked Ianto.

"A language, I think," said Toshiko, "It looks like Yngrosi to me. Or, at least, something very similar to Yngrosi."

"Oh, right." said Ianto. "And you can speak fluent Yngrosi, can you? It's just I don't remember seeing a copy of Yngrosi For Dummies knocking around anywhere..."

"No," said Toshiko, "But I've started to work out some of their writing from other artefacts we've found. Only problem is my notebook's back at my place."

Ianto stepped back.

"Oh, Tosh," he said, disapprovingly. "You know the rules about taking work home."

"It's just a notebook!" said Toshiko. "The same one that's got people's birthdays and phone numbers in it. It's hardly a breach of national security."

"But you reckon you could translate some of this stuff?" said Ianto, pointing

As they approached him, the man in the chair looked up at them both with drowsy eyes.

"Taye?" ventured Gwen, as she drew up a chair to sit beside him.

The young man nodded.

"Who're you?" he slurred.

"My name's Gwen. I'm just here to ask you a few questions."

Taye Shapiro looked from Gwen to Andy and shook his head.

"I know him," he said with a lazy snort. "He's a copper, isn't he?"

"Don't worry about him," said Gwen, smiling softly. "Now, Taye... I've been told that you know something about Mr Glee?"

Shapiro's mood changed suddenly, as he froze in his chair, his eyes growing wider with fear.

"Glee," he said, shaking his head slowly, "Glee... Glee..."

"It's okay," said Gwen. "It's okay. He's not here, Taye. We just want to know what you know, that's all."

Shapiro started laughing, nervously at first, then with increasing hysteria.

"Glee!" he cackled, "Glee!"

"What do you know about Mr Glee?" asked Gwen. "My friend says you've seen him. What does he look like, Taye?"

"Look like?" shrieked Shapiro. "You want to know what he looks like?"

Gwen nodded.

Shapiro stopped laughing very suddenly, and stared straight at Gwen, his pupils dilated to such a degree that his eyes looked almost black. He invited her closer with one gesture of his hand, and leaned forward, so that his mouth

TOSHIKO FROZE ON THE SPOT, HOLDING HER BREATH. SHE REACHED INSIDE HER JACKET AND SLID HER GUN OUT FROM ITS HOLSTER; SOMETHING SHE ALWAYS HATED DOING...

"He looks like a fish!" he bellowed, causing Gwen to jump back suddenly, nearly falling from her chair.

"Like a fish!" he screamed again, rocking back and forth in his chair. "He looks like a fish!"

From the doorway two nurses appeared, and before Gwen could say anything they were holding Shapiro down and administering a shot to his arm.

"He looks like a fish," Shapiro said, quieter now, but deadly serious. "I saw him... That's what he looks like..."

Gwen got up from her chair, and Andy held her gently by the arm.

"Seen enough?" he whispered to her.

Gwen nodded, and together they left the day room, the nurses, and the screaming of Taye Shapiro behind them.

The door closed behind her with a dull thud.

"Hi, Honey, I'm home," said Toshiko with a weary sigh, her voice echoing round the empty flat.

She kicked off her shoes, even though she knew she'd be putting them back on within minutes, and padded across the flat. There, on the living room coffee table, was an empty tub of ice cream with the spoon still in it, and next to that the open, empty DVD case of Bridget Jones's Diary. Something about the sight of the empty tub and the empty case made her sigh once more.

Toshiko would have liked somewhere with enough space for a separate study, but instead made do with one corner of the living room facing away from the television, where she kept her computer, and a bookshelf fit to bursting with textbooks, manuals, and her notebooks.

Ianto was right. She shouldn't have kept them at home, but she seriously doubted that anyone who might care to thumb through them would have the first idea what they were looking at. Her notebooks might have the odd sketch here and there, or a few symbols and hieroglyphs, but nothing that the layman would understand. Most of all, the notebooks just contained her thoughts. They weren't quite diaries – she hadn't time to keep a proper journal – just observations and feelings. She shuddered at the thought of anyone else reading them, which was why she kept them at home.

Without having to think about it, she reached up and drew out one of the identical notebooks and began leafing through its pages.

Sure enough, halfway through the book, and drawn meticulously in black ink, were the symbols written in Yngrosi, an ancient alien language, and next to them her translations. They were very basic, and possibly inaccurate in places, but they were almost identical to those Frank had said would be found on the Book of Jahi. Smiling to herself, Toshiko snapped the book shut and slid it into her pocket.

That was when she heard the front door open.

Toshiko froze on the spot, holding her breath. She reached inside her jacket and slid her gun out from its holster; something she always hated doing, even in emergencies.

"Hello?" she said. "Who's that? Jack? Owen?"

There was no reply.

She tiptoed out of the living room and into the hallway. The front door was open, and she knew for a fact she had closed it.

"Hello?" she said again, walking towards the door, both hands grasping the gun.

Toshiko opened the door a little further and looked out into the corridor to find it empty.

Satisfied that there was no one outside, she turned around on her heels to see them standing in her hallway: three creatures in pinstriped suits, their monstrous, fish-like heads each patterned with different colours.

Toshiko lifted up her gun and aimed it straight at the middle one, whom she guessed to be their ringleader.

"Get back," she said, "or I'll shoot."

The creature cackled dismissively.

"No you won't," he said, lunging forward and tearing the gun from her hands. Behind him, the other two started to laugh.

The ringleader lifted up the gun and placed it against Toshiko's head.

"Please allow me to introduce myself," he gurgled softly in her ear. "I'm Mr Glee. And these are my associates. Now come along, Miss Sato. The clock is ticking. Tick tock tick tock tick tock..."

CONTINUED ON PAGE 50!

WHERE'S YOUR HEAD AT?

BROS! BANANAS! NAKED ROLLER SKATING! SHOOTING INNOCENT PASSERS BY! EVE MYLES IS LOVELY, BUT SHE SHOULD NOT BE TRUSTED WITH FRUIT OR PELLET GUNS. READ ON TO FIND OUT WHY!

What is the full name on your birth certificate?
"Eve Myles, pure and simple."

What is your nickname?
"Mylesy. Though John Barrowman calls me Evie, and I call him Jinny."

What is your earliest memory?
"I can remember hearing the music from Tales Of The Expected, while I put on little plays with the other girls from my estate. I would have been about three years old, and I hated that music, because it meant it was Sunday night, which was always really boring. I was very theatrical even at that age, and was always wearing my mother's heels and makeup – and I knew the words to every Shirley Bassey song!"

When was your first kiss?
"I must have had my first proper kiss when I was 13. I'd pretended for months that I'd already kissed somebody else, but I never had. I remember it being horrific! My cousin told me to pretend I was chewing gum, and I used to practise on a giant Bros poster in my bedroom. I remember they all had a good going over!"

What was the last dream you had?
"I have very vivid dreams. I tend to dream about things like being on roller skates with no clothes on – those sort of anxiety dreams where everyone points and laughs at you. I'm actually quite good on roller skates in real life, but I tend not to do it naked."

When was the last time you cried?
"I cried when the last episode of Torchwood went out. I got in, had a nice bath, put my pyjamas on, got a massive cushion, turned off all the lights and I sat there and cried my eyes out!"

Do you believe in the supernatural?
"Yeah, it's nice to think that there's something other than us, to make you feel safe, isn't it? I'll always say to my mam and gramps up there, 'Take care of me today. Look after my nieces and keep my partner safe,' you know? That's the kind of supernatural I believe in."

What makes you happy?
"The sun and the sea and fish and chips." ▶

EVE MYLES

What scares you?
"The thought of losing someone I love."

What drives you mad?
"I don't really let a lot of things get to me, to be honest. Being in this profession you have to learn to let things go. But what does annoy me is when people poke their noses into other people's business and cause trouble with things that have nothing to do with them. I also can't stand it when people slurp tea!"

If you had a superpower what would it be?
"I would fly. I would hover above the Welsh rugby team and perv on them while they're all taking their clothes off. I'd be quite happy."

What was your most embarrassing experience?
"I've got plenty! Once I was sitting at a bus stop with a pretty bad hangover, so I bought myself a bottle of water and a nice big banana to make me feel better. For the life of me, I couldn't open this banana, so I bit a big chunk out of it and, of course, it turned out to be a plantain! There was an African lady sitting next to me and she was almost on her knees with laughter, watching me trying to eat this raw plantain. That was pretty embarrassing, I can tell you!"

What's the worst thing you've ever done?
"When I young, my father bought my brother a pellet gun, and when no one was around I used to hide in the apple tree behind our house and use it to shoot at

"I'D LIKE TO HOVER ABOVE THE WELSH RUGBY TEAM AND PERV ON THEM TAKING THEIR CLOTHES OFF."

anyone who came to use the phone box opposite! Eventually the police came round to confiscate the gun, and my father blamed it all on my brother! That was a long time ago, but I'm still quite a naughty person. A day doesn't go by without somebody saying, 'Oh, that naughty Eve!'"

What is you most treasured possession?
"My Torchwood contract! Or my niece, even though she's not really a possession. Other than her, I would probably have to say my surfboard. I wouldn't know what to do if something happened to that!"

What are you reading at the moment?
"At the moment I'm mainly reading scripts, actually. But the last book I read was The Lovely Bones by Alice Sebold. I almost topped myself after reading that! It was a ridiculous choice to take it on holiday and I was sobbing the whole time! You could hear me crying from miles off when I should have been having a nice time! People probably thought I was mad, but what a book!"

What are you drinking?

"Anything you've got to be 18 to buy! I especially like a nice glass of red."

Can you tell us a joke?
"Why did the boy fall off his bike? Because someone threw a fridge at him! I love that. When I first heard it in my car, I had to pull over because I was crying with laughter, but when I tell it to other people nobody ever gets it! It's rubbish, but it's brilliant!"

What is your favourite word?
"Rubbish! That is definitely my favourite word at the moment. Though possibly just because I said it a minute ago!"

What do you wish you got asked in interviews?
"Do you really want to do this interview?"

Do you really want to do this interview?
"Yes!"

What is the strangest place you've ever seen a picture of yourself?
"On the wall of a butcher's shop in Barry in South Wales. Hanging like a slab of unwanted meat!"

KISS KISS, BANG

In the beginning it was all about cold-storage snogs and girl-on-girl action in the cells, but these days the intrepid team are all paired off and settling down! Below, we take a look at Torchwood's three most enduring love stories, while over the page we connect up the teams' previous flings and fancies in the lovingly crafted Love Hub! Finally, we lick our lips at some of Torchwood's top kisses and choice chat-up lines!

THE BOSS AND THE BUTLER: JACK AND IANTO

THE FIRST MOVE

If hunting down a pterodactyl doesn't do it for you, then we don't know what will. After taking Ianto on as an employee, and saving him from his cybernetic ex with a literal kiss of life, Jack decided to mix business with pleasure and began a not-so-secret relationship with his heartbroken helpmeet.

SECOND BASE

After some late-night shifts and a stopwatch game we can only begin to envisage, Jack's death in End Of Days made Ianto realise just how much this military man meant to him. Of course, Jack came back, and the two shared their first on-screen kiss. But then Jack went AWOL with that other man in his life: the incomparable Doctor. When he returned, he had a fresh outlook on life, and asked Ianto on a proper date, just like a proper gentleman!

THE LONG HAUL

Known for his wandering eye and a relationship backstory that reads like a Who's Who of historical hotties, Jack is not the kind of guy it's easy to keep a hold on. From the moment he asked Ianto out, there was a crazy ex on the scene, and even with Captain John out of the way, who knows what else from Jack's past will come back to haunt him? Can the mild-mannered Ianto do enough to keep his man, or will he take his "innovative" dabbling elsewhere? The signs are good: It's always the quiet ones you have to watch out for!

FUTURE POTENTIAL

Jack's not getting any younger (then again, he's not getting any older, either), but after all this time he must know there's no such thing as one true love. Ianto has already been to hell and back with the loss of Lisa, so we hate to think what could happen if Jack broke his heart. Let's hope they make it work!

THE DOCTOR AND THE SCIENTIST: OWEN AND TOSH

THE FIRST MOVE

A New Year's kiss at 3am was one of many hints at Tosh's feelings for Owen, but, for his part, the intoxicated doctor could barely remember it. Despite her constant offers of support and affection, the closest Tosh got to taking Owen home with her was the photographs she had stuck up on her fridge.

SECOND BASE

After hooking up with a killer alien and a World War One soldier, Tosh finally plucked up the courage to ask Owen on a date. It's hard to say which of them was more surprised when he agreed! But Owen pulled the ultimate raincheck, by going out and getting himself killed. When he came back from the dead, devoid of his bodily functions, Tosh remained as devoted as ever, but Owen was no longer on the lookout for love.

THE LONG HAUL

When Owen had had some time to get used to the idea of being dead, he and Tosh became more like a comfortably married couple that ever before – without the complications of sex in the way. But while Tosh still held out hope against hope that a relationship might still be possible, Owen was well aware he couldn't offer her what either of them wanted. When they both stared death in the face a short time later, Owen realised just how fond of her he was, and that they never did go out for that date…

FUTURE POTENTIAL

The future's pretty bleak for these two, given that they've both kicked the bucket (two buckets in Owen's case), but if there's anything out there in the darkness, we can only hope they're making the most of it together. Older, wiser, and generally deader, Owen might at last be the loving boyfriend that Toshiko has always deserved.

BANG!

THERE'S NOTHING LIKE A DAMP UNDERGROUND BASE TO SET THE HEART AFLUTTER, SO IT CAN BE HARD TO KEEP UP WITH THE TRYSTS AND TURNS OF TORCHWOOD LOVE! .

THE WELSH LOVEBIRDS: GWEN AND RHYS

THE FIRST MOVE
The pretty PC-to-be and the future haulage transport manager met in college, where she referred to him as Rhys the Rant, and he fell for her at first sight. Like a pair of high school teenagers bickering and making-up at every opportunity, Gwen and Rhys thought they had it made, until Torchwood came along and changed everything...

SECOND BASE
It's never easy when your girlfriend is keeping secrets from you, especially when those secrets are all about aliens. With Gwen constantly putting off dinners and dates to hang out with her new colleagues, it's not surprising Rhys didn't react well to her new 'special ops' job. But he stayed the course, and was always there when she needed him most. He had no idea when she did the dirty and began an affair with Owen...

THE LONG HAUL
When Owen broke off the affair with Gwen, she came clean to Rhys to clear her conscious. His upset and outrage were short-lived, however — she had Retconned his drink so he wouldn't remember a word of her confession. She did eventually tell him the truth about Torchwood, however, and the couple were married with a promise of no more secrets. Even Gwen being pregnant with an alien baby couldn't stop them on that day!

FUTURE POTENTIAL
These two have had more ups and downs than the global economy, but with Rhys now in the loop about Torchwood, Gwen finally has someone to talk to about what really happens in her life. They've already talked about children, despite the risks of Gwen's job, so might we soon hear the sound of tiny Gwens and Rhyses, as Jack builds a playpen in the Hub?

TOSH

Poor old Tosh doesn't have much luck in love. She tends to fall for the doomed and/or dangerous, while boorish party goers and very elderly men seem to take a shine to her. Yet her strongest feelings are reserved for Owen, and go sadly unrequited until it is far too late. She is happiest, perhaps, in the false reality created by Adam, believing she is in a loving and long-term relationship. Ironically, in this illusory world, Owen adores Tosh, yet she is oblivious to him.

OWEN

When we first meet Dr Harper, he's a one-night stand kinda guy, quick to pull a girl in a bar, and no slouch about getting her boyfriend to join in, either! But, over time, we learn there's more to Owen than his playboy attitude lets on, and by the start of series two, he's thinking about settling down. He never quite gets the chance, however, making the two great loves of his life the glamorous 1950s pilot Diane, and his late fiancee, Katie, whose death broke his heart.

GWEN

Of all the team, Gwen has so far proved most successful at finding lasting love. In series one, her relationship with Rhys was looking rocky, when she got an exciting new job, developed something of a crush on her new boss Jack, and embarked on an affair with her colleague Owen. But she came to realise how much she really loved and relied on Rhys, and series two saw them engaged and then married, in defiance of all the obstacles a life with Torchwood had put in their way. Aaah!

ADAM SMITH

Messed with Tosh's mind to make her believe she had been in a two-year relationship with him. It made her happier and more confident than she had ever been, but it was all a lie, and the truth was soon discovered.
(Adam)

DIANE HOLMES

After Katie, this displaced 1950s pilot is the first woman to get through to the real Owen – capable of love and not just lust. Though she loves him, too, she longs for her own time, and leaves him heartbroken in a desperate attempt to go back through the Rift.
(Out Of Time)

KATIE RUSSELL

Owen's fiancée before he joined Torchwood was thought to suffer from early onset Alzheimer's, but was in fact the victim of an alien parasite attached to her brain. Owen did everything he could to save the woman he loved, but she died in surgery, leaving him broken, angry and afraid of commitment.
(Fragments)

RHYS WILLIAMS

Rugged, reliable Rhys may not save the world on a regular basis, but he's always there for Gwen at the end of the day. He fancied her from the moment they met at college, and despite some rocky moments along the way, the pair eventually got married.

TOMMY BROCKLESS

Frozen in 1918, Tommy melted Toshiko's heart in the present day. She had to wait a year for each meeting with him, but eventually they spent the night together, before he sacrificed himself to save the world.
(To The Last Man)

SUZIE COSTELLO

As a feisty and attractive member of the team, it comes as no surprise to learn that Suzie once had an affair with Owen...
(They Keep Killing Suzie)

CARYS FLETCHER

Reduced Gwen to a frenzy of snogging, thanks to the alien pheromones she was giving off, and subsequently left Owen somewhat exposed...
(Day One)

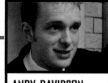

ANDY DAVIDSON

Like a faithful puppy, PC Andy has adored Gwen through thick and thin. So jealous of Rhys, he couldn't even bear to attend Gwen's wedding, he still stands by Gwen in times of need.
(Adrift and others)

BANANA BOAT

HENRY PARKER

MARY

Hits on Tosh in a bar, but is not what she seems. An alien criminal in a stolen body, she uses her charms to seduce Tosh and infiltrate Torchwood. Tosh, who has never kissed a girl before, starts a relationship with Mary (and finds out she is an alien), only to be betrayed.
(Greeks Bearing Gifts)

NIGHTCLUB COUPLE

With a little help from an alien aphrodisiac, Owen takes these two home after trying it on in a bar.
(Everything Changes)

MARTHA JONES

Though happily seeing Dr Tom Milligan by this point, Martha is amused by Owen's flirting, and can't help but snog Jack before leaving Cardiff.
(Reset, Dead Man Walking, A Day In The Death)

EUGENE JONES

Worshipped Gwen from afar, but it wasn't until he died that he got to spend some time with her. Though she didn't know he was there, she grew to admire him, and they even kissed before he left this life for good.
(Random Shoes)

JACK

Captain Jack Harkness has always been a passionate man, but since he learned he could not stay dead, he has had to deal with more loss than most of us could bear, as those around him aged and died. Though this has made him wary of developing new attachments, his head is still turned from time to time, and he has never forgotten how to flirt like a pro. We know he's been married at least once before, and recently he's allowed Ianto into his life in a big way. Let's hope it works out for them!

IANTO

Unlike his colleagues, Ianto had barely a snog in the first series of Torchwood, being a thoroughly devoted and loyal lover at all times. Unfortunately for him, his first devotion was to part Cyber-converted Lisa, whom he kept hidden in the depths of the Hub. His secret and hopeless love gnawed away at him, until it was discovered by the team. After that, he embarked on a process of renewal, that saw him acting on an attraction to Jack he had felt since the first time they met.

MYSTERY WIFE

At the bottom of a box of photos and keepsakes is Jack's faded, sepia wedding photo. Who is his bride on this happy day? Only he remembers now, and he's not saying! (Something Borrowed)

ESTELLE COLE

Jack's World War Two sweetheart still remembers him fondly in her old age, though she believes the man she knows in the 21st Century is the son of the lover she knew in the 1940s. For his part, Jack still loves her and looks out for her, but he is too late to save her life from malevolent fairies. (Small Worlds)

CAPTAIN JOHN

They were only together for two weeks, but that's a very long time when you're stuck in a time loop! Jack and John clearly shared a very passionate relationship, but John's influence was not a good one, and Jack moved on while John did not... (Kiss Kiss, Bang Bang and Exit Wounds)

LISA HALLETT

Got together with Ianto when they both worked at Torchwood One in London. Though recorded as dead in the Battle of Canary Wharf, she was in fact left part converted into a Cyberman. Ianto desperately tried to keep her body alive, but her mind and emotions were slowly lost to the Cyber technology. He was unable to come to terms with the fact she was gone, and was willing to risk every life on Earth rather than give up on her. (Cyberwoman)

JACK HARKNESS

Sparks fly when Jack meets Jack! The 51st Century Captain never met his 1940s namesake until a time slip sent him back to 1941. There, knowing that this other Jack would die the next day, our own Jack defied the sensibilities of the day to act upon their mutual attraction. (Captain Jack Harkness)

THE DOCTOR

In many ways, Jack and the Doctor would be perfect for each other, but, apart from planting a big kiss on the ninth Doctor's lips, Jack kept his feelings for the Time Lord to himself.

LOTS OF OTHERS!

Jack finds most time for flirting when relieved of the burden of leadership. During his travels with the Doctor and Rose, he took a shine to someone almost everywhere he went, from members of staff on the Gamestation, to the alien Chantho. (Doctor Who, Utopia and others)

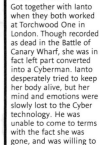

A POODLE

DETECTIVE SWANSON

Wasn't impressed with Torchwood's methods, but was still not immune to Jack's flirtatious offer to strip for her! (They Keep Killing Suzie)

RECEPTIONIST RUTH

Another notch on Jack's big flirting stick, Ruth must dream of the day Jack will whisk her away from Harwood's Haulage! (Meat)

ALICE GUPPY

Couldn't help but notice Jack was cute, but still thought Emily cuter! What is it with these irresistible Torchwood bosses? (Fragments)

EMILY HOLROYD

KEY

LOVERS

NO STRINGS

SECRET ADMIRER

PASSING FANCY

IT'S COMPLICATED

⟷ MUTUAL FEELINGS

→ ONE-WAY FEELINGS

Greeks Bearing Gifts

SIX OF THE BEST

HALF A DOZEN CRACKING SMACKERS FROM THE TONGUE-TWISTING TORCHWOOD TEAM!

JUST CHILLIN'
GWEN AND OWEN (CYBERWOMAN)

When there's a Cyberwoman on the loose, the only thing for Gwen and Owen to do is squeeze into a cold storage locker, even if it means Gwen going on top! Certain his life is about to end at the metallic hands of a bikini-clad monster, Owen goes in for the kill and kisses Gwen, much to her surprise. It's only when he realises they're not going to die that he feels a bit embarrassed about getting quite so excited.

HOTHOUSE HEAT
JACK AND IANTO (ADRIFT)

If anyone's going to take the crown for getting hot and bothered in the Hub, it has to be Jack and Ianto. After a hard day at work, they can always find time for a game of naked hide-and-seek or a stop-off in the office with a stopwatch. We see them enjoy a full-on snog in the heat of the moment in To The Last Man, but it's not until Gwen walks in on them in the hothouse that we really get an insight into their gardening habits!

ALIEN ATTRACTION
TOSH AND MARY (GREEKS BEARING GIFTS)

When Mary's mind-reading pendant lets Tosh hear her thoughts, Mary makes sure that they're worth listening in to! And so, sure of Mary's romantic intentions towards her, Tosh puts aside her usual self doubt, and the two of them kiss with the innocence and enthusiasm of schoolgirls! Of course, Mary turns out to be not quite so innocent, but it's nice to see Tosh getting some action once in a while!

STERN AND STEAMY
JACK AND JOHN (KISS KISS, BANG BANG)

Jack had only been back in town a few hours before his rollercoaster life cranked into action once more! Summoned to a bar by his old flame John, the two waste no time in swapping sucker punches or saliva! Sci-fi fans could hardly believe their eyes! That guy from Buffy was making out with that guy from Doctor Who! What was going on? Was it some beautiful dream? No, it was the return of Torchwood, of course!

TRUE LOVE
GWEN AND RHYS (SOMETHING BORROWED)

There were times when it seemed these two might never make it down the aisle, but secret lives, memory loss and alien insemination were no match for this indomitable pair! When they finally got hitched, it was a moment to remember. Battered and bruised like no bride and groom before them, they took a moment to forget all their Torchwood-based troubles with a lingering and heartfelt kiss to seal the deal!

KISS OF LIFE
JACK AND CARYS (DAY ONE)

It may not be filled with passion, but when Jack kisses Carys to save her life, it's a gesture that's certainly given with love. A golden glow passes from his mouth to hers, and she gasps with life that we thought she'd lost. We've all had great kisses from time to time, but the truly life-saving lip-smacker is a thing to behold. We wonder if Ianto gets an extra 20 years or so, every time he gets to push with the Captain?

TORCH-WOO!
CHOICE CHAT-UP LINES, TORCHWOOD STYLE!

THE DIRECT APPROACH...

Carys: "There's nothing else out there like it. You taste so good. You're the best hit there is." (Day One)

Detective Swanson: "Tell me something. Are you always this dressy for a murder investigation?"
Jack: "What, would you rather me naked?" (They Keep Killing Suzie)

Jack: "This is the entrance for tourists."
John: "I remember the last time you said that." (Kiss Kiss, Bang Bang)

Owen: "We could go back to mine, read up about yourself on the net... That sounds like a line. It's not a line. I'm not chatting you up." (Out Of Time)

Owen: "What? It's not like I fancy you or anything."
Gwen: "I was lying on top of you; I could feel your hard-on." (Cyberwoman)

THE TROUBLE WITH LOVE...

Lisa (to Ianto): "Transplant my brain into your body. We will be one complete person. Isn't that what love is?" (Cyberwoman)

Rhys (to Gwen): "I thought, I'm going to marry this bloody mad woman, even if it kills me!" (Adam)

Gwen: "It's not about the money, Rhys! I want to marry you today, whatever happens. If the skies suddenly fill with spaceships, or an army of Weevils climb out of the drains on St Mary Street, you fool!" (Something Borrowed)

Alternative Owen: "I've got so much love to give you Tosh, and you won't know that unless I tell you. So here I am, telling you that I love you." (Adam)

TREAT 'EM MEAN...

Gwen: "You are unbelievable!"
John: "And yet you find me strangely attractive..." (Kiss Kiss, Bang Bang)

Gwen (to Rhys): "I'm ashamed! And I'm angry! And I want... I need you to forgive me. And, because I've drugged you." (Combat)

Banana Boat: "I'm Banana! Suppose you can tell why?"
Tosh: "You come up in spots and go soft quickly?"
Banana Boat: "Actually, I'm the best man."
Tosh: "Evolution is full of surprises." (Something Borrowed)

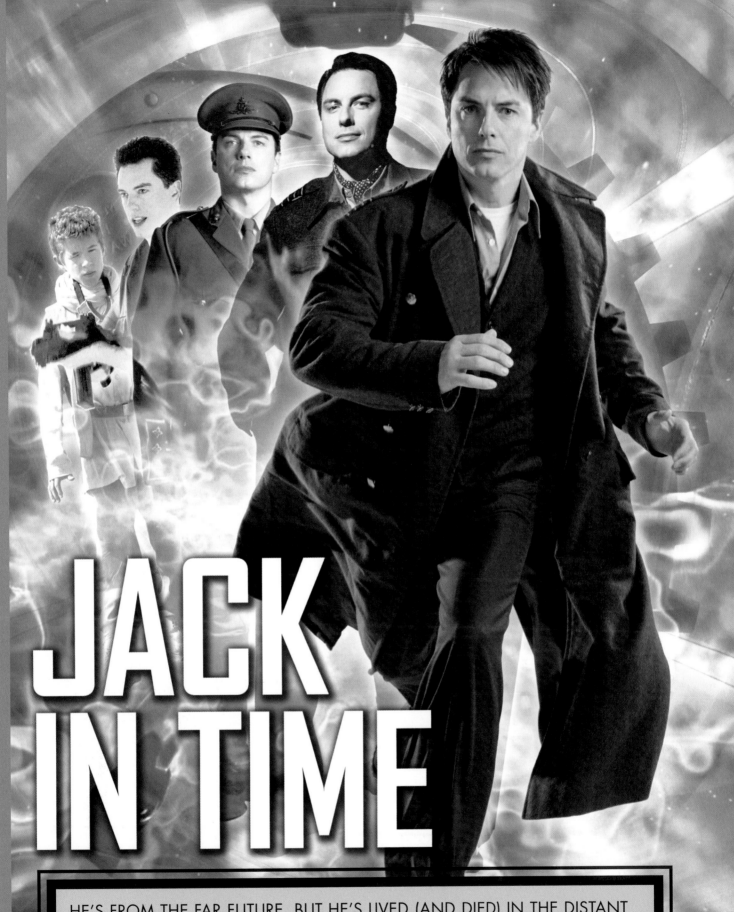

JACK IN TIME

HE'S FROM THE FAR FUTURE, BUT HE'S LIVED (AND DIED) IN THE DISTANT PAST. NOW HE PROTECTS US FROM BOTH IN PRESENT DAY CARDIFF... TIME TO UNTANGLE JACK'S TUMULTUOUS TIMELINE, WE RECKON!

TIMELINE 1: BIRTH TO AGE 65 (APPROX.)

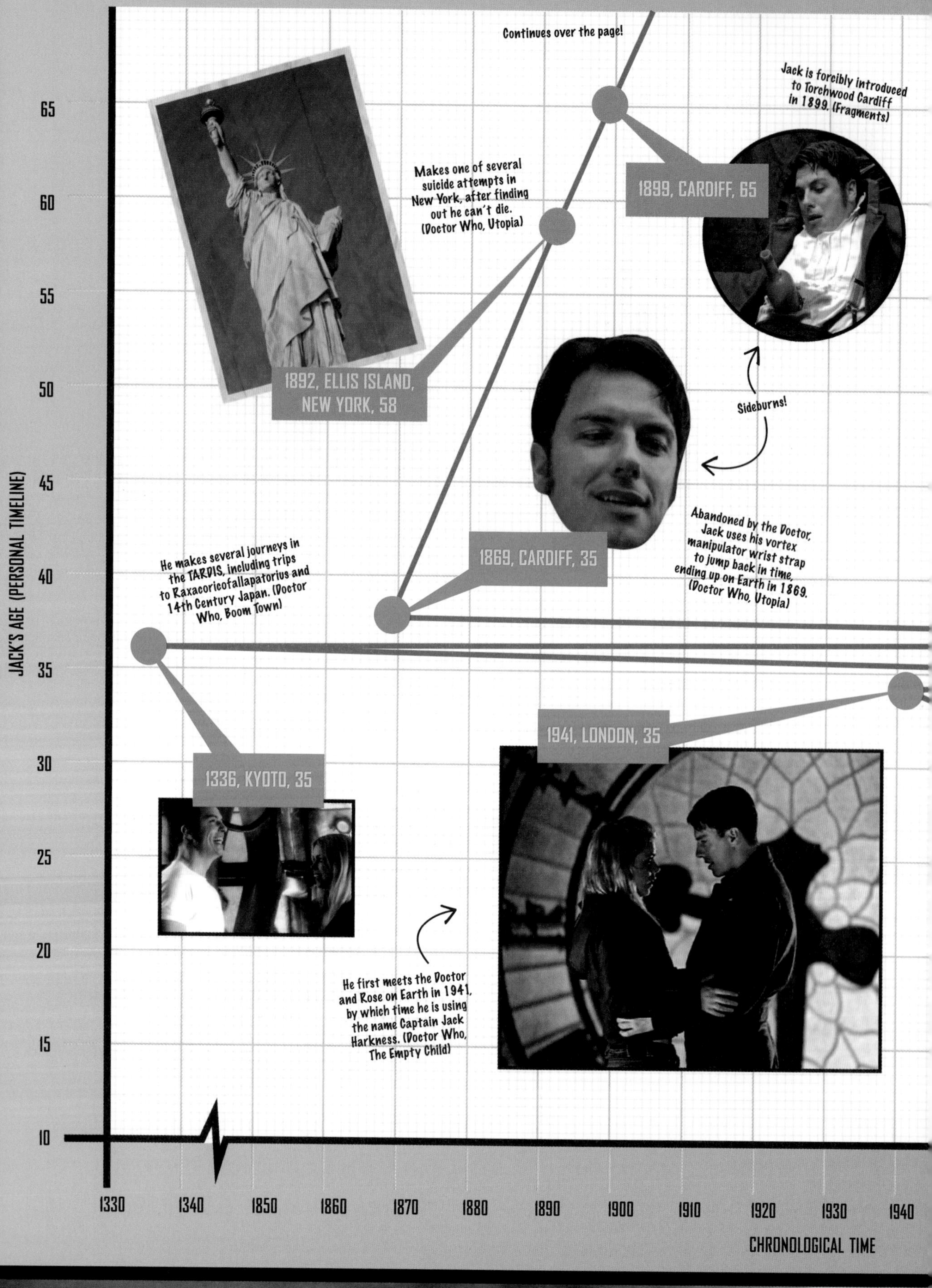

Continues over the page!

Jack is forcibly introduced to Torchwood Cardiff in 1899. (Fragments)

1899, CARDIFF, 65

Makes one of several suicide attempts in New York, after finding out he can't die. (Doctor Who, Utopia)

Sideburns!

1892, ELLIS ISLAND, NEW YORK, 58

Abandoned by the Doctor, Jack uses his vortex manipulator wrist strap to jump back in time, ending up on Earth in 1869. (Doctor Who, Utopia)

1869, CARDIFF, 35

He makes several journeys in the TARDIS, including trips to Raxacoricofallapatorius and 14th Century Japan. (Doctor Who, Boom Town)

1941, LONDON, 35

1336, KYOTO, 35

He first meets the Doctor and Rose on Earth in 1941, by which time he is using the name Captain Jack Harkness. (Doctor Who, The Empty Child)

JACK'S AGE (PERSONAL TIMELINE)

65
60
55
50
45
40
35
30
25
20
15
10

1330 1340 1850 1860 1870 1880 1890 1900 1910 1920 1930 1940

CHRONOLOGICAL TIME

Jack's journey begins at the bottom right of this page, when he is born and raised in the 51st Century. His idyllic childhood is shattered at some point in his teens, after which he joins the Time Agency. As a Time Agent, and subsequently as a companion of the Doctor, he travels to many times and places, of which we know only a few. Abandoned by the Doctor in 200,100, Jack uses his vortex manipulator to travel to 1869, and lives out the century on Earth.

Exterminate!

Disclaimer! This timeline is far from complete, and includes only what we know about Jack's life so far. All ages are approximate, and Jack could, in fact, be much older, as he could pop out for a century of adventures at any time, and we might never know!

His last regular journey with the Doctor is to the Game Station in the year 200,100, where he is exterminated by a Dalek, before being brought back to life by an unwitting Rose. From this point on, he cannot die. (Doctor Who, The Parting Of The Ways)

200,100, GAME STATION, EARTH ORBIT, 35

We reckon Jack's about 35 during this whole middle bit, but we've spaced it out to make it clearer.

2006, CARDIFF AND RAXACORICOFALLAPATORIUS, 35

Argh!

Jack has a happy childhood, until his homeworld is attacked in his teens. (Adam)

As a young adult, Jack joins the Time Agency, and presumably makes many short trips back and forth in time during his 20s and early 30s.

Start Here >

51ST CENTURY, BOESHANE PENINSULA, AGED 15

| 1960 | 1970 | 1980 | 1990 | 2000 | 2010 | 2020 | 2030 | 2040 | 2050 | 5000 | 200,000 |

TIMELINE 2: AGE 65 TO 2,158 (APPROX.)

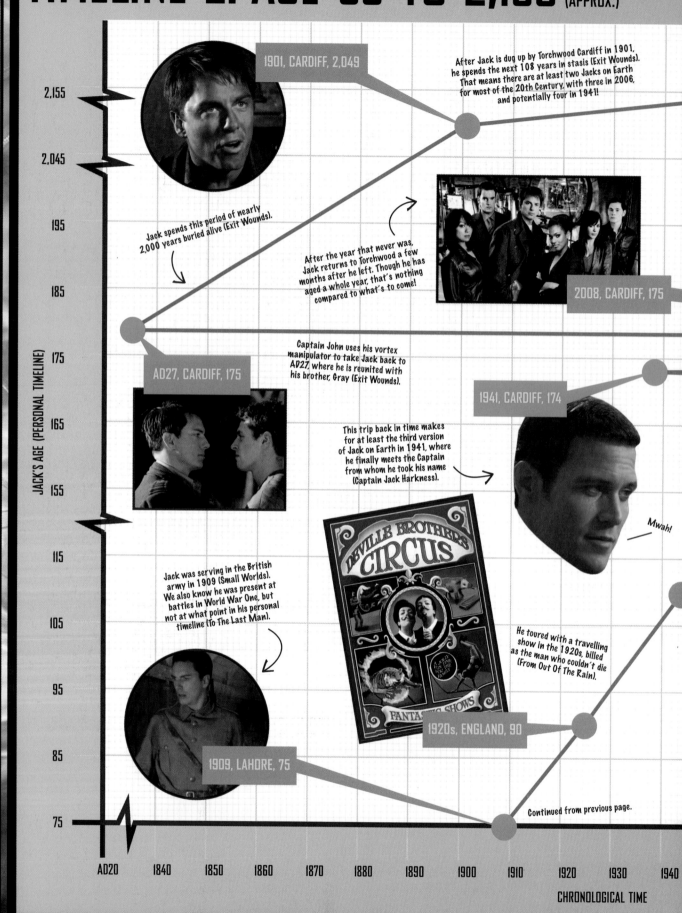

2,155
2,045
195
185
175
165
155
115
105
95
85
75

JACK'S AGE (PERSONAL TIMELINE)

1901, CARDIFF, 2,049

After Jack is dug up by Torchwood Cardiff in 1901, he spends the next 108 years in stasis (Exit Wounds). That means there are at least two Jacks on Earth for most of the 20th Century, with three in 2006, and potentially four in 1941!

Jack spends this period of nearly 2,000 years buried alive (Exit Wounds).

After the year that never was, Jack returns to Torchwood a few months after he left. Though he has aged a whole year, that's nothing compared to what's to come!

2008, CARDIFF, 175

AD27, CARDIFF, 175

Captain John uses his vortex manipulator to take Jack back to AD27, where he is reunited with his brother, Gray (Exit Wounds).

1941, CARDIFF, 174

This trip back in time makes for at least the third version of Jack on Earth in 1941, where he finally meets the Captain from whom he took his name (Captain Jack Harkness).

Mwah!

Jack was serving in the British army in 1909 (Small Worlds). We also know he was present at battles in World War One, but not at what point in his personal timeline (To The Last Man).

DEVILLE BROTHERS CIRCUS
FANTASTIC SHOWS

He toured with a travelling show in the 1920s, billed as the man who couldn't die (From Out Of The Rain).

1920s, ENGLAND, 90

1909, LAHORE, 75

Continued from previous page.

AD20   1840   1850   1860   1870   1880   1890   1900   1910   1920   1930   1940

CHRONOLOGICAL TIME

This is where Jack's timeline starts to get really complicated! He crops up a few times during the 20th Century, including during both World Wars, but the 21st Century is when everything changes! Suddenly, he's pinging back and forth from the end of the universe to the dawn of the Common Era, experiencing years that never happened and crossing his own timeline like nobody's business! Where the graph goes after this, we can but guess...

After waking from stasis just a short time after he was taken back to AD27 by Captain John (Exit Wounds), Jack saw in 2009 revived and refreshed for the rest of the 21st Century, and whatever new adventures await!

2008, CARDIFF, 2,158

Jack returns to 21st Century Earth with the Doctor and Martha Jones, using his vortex manipulator. There, they live through a year that is subsequently wiped from history, though not from their own experience (Doctor Who, The Sound Of Drums, The Last Of The Time Lords).

2008, LONDON, 174

100 TRILLION, MALCASSAIRO, 174

Takes a trip to the end of the universe, clinging on to the outside of the TARDIS! (Doctor Who, Utopia)

Inherits Torchwood Cardiff after a century's faithful service on New Year's Eve, 1999, after leader Alex Hopkins kills himself and his team. (Fragments).

Returns to 2008 after his trip to 1941 (Captain Jack Harkness).

2008, CARDIFF, 174

1999/2000 CARDIFF, 166

Jack meets Estelle Cole while living through World War Two for at least the second time (Small Worlds).

2008, CARDIFF, 174

1990S, POWELL ESTATE, LONDON, 157-166

1943, LONDON, 109

Watching over Rose Tyler as she grows up (Doctor Who, Utopia).

50   1960   1970   1980   1990   2000   2010   100 TRILLION

TOSH?" JACK'S VOICE ECHOED INSIDE TOSHIKO'S apartment. The door had been left open, but there was no sign of her inside. Further down the hallway, Ianto checked the last room. "Nothing," he said.

"Okay," said Jack, and then, speaking into his headset, "Owen, we're at Tosh's apartment. She's gone."

There was a long pause at the other end of the line before Owen spoke. "Really?" he said.

"Yes... Really. You need to check that Kelly Jenkins is okay. If Tosh has gone..."

"Seriously, Jack... Kelly's not my number one fan right now..."

"Just check. Please."

"Okay. Whatever you say."

As the line went quiet once more, Jack and Ianto heard footsteps in the corridor outside. They turned quickly, guns ready, to see Gwen standing in the doorway.

"She's not here?" said Gwen.

"No," replied Jack. "We need to get to Cwmblaidd."

"Why now? We need to find Tosh."

"If they've got Tosh then there's a chance they know where the Book is, and they'll have taken her there. It's our best chance of finding her."

Gwen and Ianto nodded. They knew Jack was right. Cwmblaidd, the now deserted town where Frank Jenkins had hidden the Book of Jahi, would be under millions of gallons of water within a matter of hours – flooded to form an enormous reservoir. Gaunt with worry, they followed Jack out of Tosh's apartment, and together they ran back to the SUV.

Driving them away from the apartment block, Jack turned his attention to Ianto.

"So," he said, "Mr Glee... What have we got?"

"Well," Ianto replied, "He's a name that crops up time and time again, going back as far as the 1920s, when he supposedly ran a bordello in Bute Town. Since then he's had his hand in everything going, from black market nylons to smuggling cocaine."

"Okay. Gwen: did you find anything?"

"Yes," said Gwen, bluntly. "It turns out he's a fish."

There was a long silence, but for the growl of the SUV's engine.

"A fish?" asked Jack. "You mean he's one of those Blowfish guys?"

"Unless we've got any other species of criminal fish lording it over the Cardiff underworld," said Gwen.

"Like a sort of Codfather?" ventured Ianto, to very little response.

Jack turned a sharp corner, then spoke into his headset once more.

"Owen... Have we got anything from Kelly?"

"Nothing, Jack. She's not answering."

"Okay... You stay at the Hub. We're going to Cwmblaidd."

"*Cwmblaidd*?" said Owen. "You mean you're not picking me up first?"

"No," said Jack. "You've had more than enough excitement, given your current condition. Besides, we need someone to give us satellite back-up."

"But Jack, if they've got Tosh..."

"It's an order, Owen, not a request. We've only got another five hours before they flood that valley, and we need you in the Hub."

There was a long silence on the line before Owen answered.

"Yes, Jack," he said.

THE BOOK OF

G wen had been to Cwmblaidd before, in her childhood. An old mining town that had seen better days, Cwmblaidd was never the most glamorous of places, but nothing prepared her for the shock of seeing it so utterly deserted.

It was impossible to drive into the town itself. The road leading down from the mountainside was cut off abruptly by a large wire fence and gates. Jack parked the SUV, and he, Gwen and Ianto climbed out.

Much of the town had been demolished to make way for the reservoir. Row after row of terraced houses that had stood for a century or more, now razed to the ground leaving brown scars down both sides of the valley. Further down was a colossal dam, an impenetrable wall of dark grey concrete, rising ominously above Cwmblaidd.

"Okay," said Ianto, gripping the fence and shaking it vigorously. "What now?"

Jack studied the gate for a moment, then reached in to his coat, producing a small key which he used to unlock the gate in seconds.

"What's that?" asked Ianto. "Alien tech?"

"No," said Jack, holding up the skeleton key. "Parisian tech. Picked this up during the riots in '68."

"I won't even ask..." said Gwen, turning back to the SUV.

"Wait up, Gwen. We walk from here," said Jack. "Ianto, you stay here with the SUV and let us know if anyone's heading this way."

"But Jack!" said Gwen. "It's *miles* to Frank's flat."

"I know," said Jack. "But we won't get there by car."

Looking past the gates, Gwen saw enormous concrete blocks scattered in the road, too large and close together for the SUV to pass.

As Jack and Gwen passed through the gate, Jack turned to Ianto with one more instruction.

"If the floodgates open, you drive away."

"But—" Ianto began.

"No buts. Just drive. This whole valley will be under water by sunrise. If we're not out when the floodgates open, we won't get out at all."

N obody had spoken in a long time, and Toshiko had spent the journey so far blindfolded. When the blindfold was removed, she saw the inside of a limousine. It was travelling along a dual ▶

JAHI PART 3
BY DAVID LLEWELLYN
ILLUSTRATIONS MIKE DOWLING

carriageway near the outskirts of the city, and she was sat beside one of the Blowfish, who had a gun aimed squarely at her side. Facing them in the rear passenger seats were Mr Glee and Kelly Jenkins. A third Blowfish, sat in the front, was driving.

"Kelly!" said Toshiko. "They got you, too?"

"You stupid woman," snapped Kelly. "Who do you think told them where Frank put the Book?"

"What?" asked Toshiko. "But how did you—"

"That friend of yours?" Kelly interrupted, raising one sassy eyebrow. "The one who fancies himself as a bit of a ladies' man?"

"Owen?"

"Yeah. That's him. He told me *all* about it."

Toshiko shook her head in dismay. How could Owen be so stupid?

She sighed. He hadn't been stupid. Gullible, maybe, but not stupid. How could he have known Kelly was working for Mr Glee?

"But why?" she asked, after a long pause. "Why would you do this?"

Kelly laughed.

"Why?" she said, sarcastically. "Money, of course. Frank had tons of the stuff but he was tighter than a snare drum. Besides, he was old and I was bored. A girl needs a little excitement, if you know what I mean."

Toshiko looked down to see Mr Glee's hand on Kelly's knee.

"Oh," she said with a grimace, "that's just disgusting."

"Hey, girlfriend," said Kelly. "Don't knock it 'til you've tried it."

Ianto opened the door and jumped out of the SUV. Sure enough, somewhere beyond a bend in the mountain road he heard the engine of another car and saw the glow of its headlights flickering through the trees. He took a deep breath and drew his gun from its holster, as the sound of the approaching car grew louder.

The twin beams of the headlights flashed up and over the brow of the hill so that they shone straight at him, and he shielded his eyes with his arm. Seconds later the car screeched to a halt when its bumper was only a few feet away from his shins.

Ianto breathed out.

He heard the car doors open and close with a loud clunk and saw shadowy figures making their way toward him. One of the car's occupants stepped into the light, and he saw instantly that it was a creature in a pinstriped suit, its amphibious head covered with black and red stripes.

"You must be the errand boy," said the creature, with a guttural laugh that rattled in the back of its throat.

The other figures stepped into the light, and Ianto saw Kelly Jenkins and two more Blowfish, one of whom had Toshiko by the throat with a gun to her head.

"I'm Mr Glee," said the Blowfish with the red and black markings. "I suggest you drop your weapon."

Ianto glanced over at Toshiko. She looked terrified. What could he do? Closing his eyes and silently cursing himself, Ianto dropped his gun to the ground, where it fell with a loud clatter.

TOSH LOOKED DOWN TO SEE MR GLEE'S HAND ON KELLY'S KNEE, AND GRIMACED. "HEY, GIRLFRIEND," SAID KELLY. "DON'T KNOCK IT 'TIL YOU'VE TRIED IT."

Gwen had never felt so claustrophobic in so open a space before. Though the valley was wide enough, it very suddenly seemed so oppressive, the dark mountains on either side rising up and narrowing the black night sky. If there hadn't been a full moon, neither she nor Jack could have seen a thing, the street lights having been removed some time ago, leaving gaping wounds in every pavement.

On the edges of the town they passed a primary school, one of the few buildings this far out that hadn't been demolished. A foam-covered climbing frame stood skeletal in the centre of a deserted playground, while crayon stick figure families gazed blankly from the windows of an empty classroom.

"It's so weird," said Gwen. "This was a town. These were people's houses, and the schools where they sent their kids. Now look at it..."

"Happens to all places eventually," said Jack, "You know anyone who's taken a holiday to Rhodes?"

"Er, yes," said Gwen. "My aunty. Years ago. Why?"

"Did she get any photos of the Colossus?"

"Er... no?"

"Well there you go," said Jack, "Nothing lasts forever, Gwen. Nothing."

"Ianto!" Jumping with shock, his hands braced on the steering wheel, Ianto looked down at the speakers; the source of Owen's disembodied voice.

"Ianto. Are you there?"

"I'm here."

"Listen... There's another vehicle coming down Llanfroo... I'm sorry, I can't pronounce the name of the road. Too many L's and not enough vowels. But there's a car coming down the road toward the town. It's heading your way."

"Really?"

"Yeah. Doesn't look like a maintenance vehicle of any sort. Keep your eyes peeled. It'll be with you in about 30 seconds."

"Good boy," said Mr Glee, drawing his own gun and crossing over to Ianto, pushing its barrel into his cheek.

"Down," growled Glee. "Now."

Ianto nodded, and fell to his knees. His eyes shut tight and his heart pounding a little faster, he heard the gun's hammer being drawn back and the bullet clicking into its chamber.

"No!" said Toshiko. "If you kill him you'll never know how the Book works. I'm the only one who can read the markings on it."

Ianto opened his eyes and looked up at Toshiko. She smiled at him weakly, though there were tears in her eyes, and Ianto laughed nervously and smiled back.

"As you wish," said Mr Glee, lifting up his gun and slamming it against Ianto's head. Ianto lurched sideways and fell at the creature's feet, unconscious.

"No!" screamed Toshiko.

Glee crouched down on his haunches and pressed two scaly fingers against Ianto's throat.

"He's still alive," he said, standing once more. "See? I'm a man of my word. Now come along. We haven't much time."

They were on the high street. The shop fronts were boarded up; signs that had been backlit now dim and lifeless. Gwen had to remind herself that outside of this valley the rest of the world was still going about its business. It was all too easy to imagine, in this deserted town, that she and Jack were the last people on Earth.

A plane rumbled overhead, leaving a jet trail lit up silver by the light of the moon, and somewhere in the shadows two abandoned cats fought, mewling and howling before a sudden clatter and smash of glass sent them scurrying away, unseen.

As they neared the end of the high street, Gwen kicked at something on ▶

the ground
and looked down to
see a plastic doll lying in the
gutter. She paused for a moment,
gazing into its lifeless plastic eyes, and felt an
overwhelming sadness. She imagined its owner,
now living in the temporary town at Sunny Bay, wondering
where the doll could be. Gwen took a deep breath, and walked on,
quickening her pace to catch up with Jack.

The metal sign for "PLATFORM 1" swung back and forth on its chains, creaking noisily over the whispering breeze. Kelly led the way along what had been train tracks between the platforms of the disused station, with the three Blowfish and Toshiko close behind.

The station buildings were empty; the paint on their wooden cladding peeling away. Out-of-date posters advertising paperback novels and touring productions of West End shows still hung in vandalised frames.

As they climbed up onto the platform and walked on into the station itself, Toshiko looked up at Mr Glee.

"What I'd like to know," she asked, "is why? Why do you want the Book in the first place? What good is it to someone like you?"

Mr Glee leered at her over his shoulder, the spines on his head rising up.

"It's all about expansion," he replied coldly. "This world's too small for the likes of us. There are so many opportunities in other times and on other worlds. Imagine if you could take a submachine gun to ancient Rome or Byzantium. You'd be a god within hours. Or how about introducing heroin to medieval England? You'd have the market to yourself. Forget the world... The *universe* would be your oyster."

"So you'd kill people or make them addicts," snapped Toshiko, "just for your own profit?"

Mr Glee laughed.

"You seem offended," he said, still laughing. "I'm sure in that pretty little head of yours the world is run by kind and generous people whose only concern is the welfare of others. Well, you can help yourself to that delusion. The real world – no, *all* worlds – are run by those who seize them for all their worth. Moral dilemmas are for children and paupers, and I am neither."

He turned his back to her, and Kelly led them out through the station's exit and onto a long and empty street. At the end of the street stood a towering block of flats.

"Ah," said Glee, clapping his hands together, "we're nearly home."

This was when he should have been drinking endless cups of coffee. This was when his pulse should have been racing and his every breath shorter than the last. If he'd ever taken up smoking, this was when he would have chained his way through a pack of 20. Of course, none of those things were possible, because Owen Harper was technically dead.

Even so, the dead man sat hunched over his console, tapping at keys and patching himself through to Jack's headset.

"Owen..."

"Jack... we have a problem."

"What is it?"

"Another car just came down Llan... Llanfroo... It's just come down the main road into Cwmblaidd. I warned Ianto it was coming, and now I can't get hold of him. The line's gone dead."

There was a long pause. All Owen could hear was the faint crackle of static on the line and the dank drip, drip, drip of water inside the Hub.

"Okay," said Jack, eventually. "Anything else?"

"You *could* say that..."

Owen looked up at his screen. In the centre of it was a satellite heat vision image of Cwmblaidd. Making their way through the deserted town, Jack and Gwen showed up as no more than two white specks, twinkling in the darkness. Not far from them, Owen saw five more specks, three of them a little dimmer than the others.

"You've got company," said Owen. "Five people. I'm pretty sure one of them's Tosh."

"Are they all human?" asked Jack.

"Not sure. They're cutting across town. Looks like one of them knows a shortcut, because they've got a lead on you..."

"Okay, Owen..."

Jack was about to say something, but the line began to break up.

"If... y... Gwe... eyes... street... g..."

"Typical!" said Owen, slamming his fist against the desk.

This was when he would have held his breath.

Bevan House was as tall as it was ugly, rising 10 storeys above a rabbits' warren of smaller blocks. Gwen wouldn't say anything to Jack, but just the sight of all these empty buildings, with not a single window illuminated from the inside, gave her goosebumps. The further across Cwmblaidd they had walked, the more and more Gwen had felt the absence of human life in the valley. The only living things were creatures that scurried and screeched in the shadows.

They came to the entrance of Bevan House to find the door ripped from its hinges and lying flat inside the lobby.

"Which floor did Frank live on?" asked Gwen.

place reeked of damp and decay, as if in the absence of organic matter, the building itself was rotting around them.

Silently they made their way along the corridor until they reached a door that, unlike the others, had been left ajar. Jack turned to Gwen, nodded, and Gwen in turn lifted her gun, and nudged the door open with one foot. From inside the flat they heard the sound of splintering wood. Jack nodded again, and he and Gwen entered the flat.

"Ah, Harkness," said a voice from the shadows. "I wondered when you would join us."

It took a moment for their eyes to adjust to the gloom, but soon enough both Gwen and Jack saw the three Blowfish, Kelly Jenkins, and Toshiko. One of the three aliens was crouching beside a hole in the floorboards and lifting out a small brown box, no larger than a laptop computer, and covered in countless buttons and dials.

It was the Book of Jahi.

A second Blowfish had Toshiko in a vice-like grip, his gun held against the side of her head.

The creature who had spoken stepped forward into the moonlight, aiming his pistol at Gwen.

"I'd drop your guns if I were you," he said to Jack. "Or the girls get it."

"Mr Glee, I presume," hissed Jack.

"Very astute," replied Mr Glee. "Now drop the guns."

Jack looked from Toshiko to Gwen, sighed, and placed his gun very carefully on the ground, gesturing for Gwen to do the same.

"Boys," said Mr Glee, "take Miss Sato back to the car. Kelly, you go with them."

The two Blowfish and Kelly nodded in turn and then left, dragging Toshiko with them. Mr Glee backed his way toward the door.

"And don't even *think* about following us," he said, "I think you'll find all the exits blocked."

He reached inside his jacket and pulled out a hand grenade.

"A wonderful invention," he said. "They really are an inventive bunch, these humans. Such a shame your little apprentice here won't live, really, but such is life. TTFN."

Cackling to himself, Glee slammed the door shut and they heard his footfalls as he ran from the flat and down the stairwell. Seconds later there was a deafening bang and the sound of smashing glass and falling concrete.

Gwen covered her ears.

"What was *that*?" she shouted over the noise.

"That," yelled Jack, "was the stairs."

"So what are we gonna do?"

Jack picked up his gun and slid it back into its holster. He looked out through the living room window at the night sky, and then at Gwen.

"Jack... What are you thinking, Jack?"

Without saying a word Jack picked up an old wooden chair from one corner of the room.

"Jack... Tell me, Jack... What are you—"

Without answering her, Jack threw the chair through the window, shattering the pane in an instant.

"Okay," he said, turning to Gwen. "Think of me as your cushion."

"What? No, Jack. Seriously... We're seven storeys up. Are you *insane*? Jack... I'm getting *married*. What if this goes wrong? Rhys'll kill you. Several times over. And I won't be around to stop him, Jack..."

"Come on," said Jack, climbing up into the window frame, and grinning from ear to ear. "It'll be fine. Trust me." ▶

"Seventh," replied Jack.

"Typical," sighed Gwen. "I don't suppose the lifts are working?"

"No," Jack laughed.

"Honestly, Jack... Two blocks of flats in one day and not a working bloody elevator between them."

"Well you could always wait down here," said Jack, with a grin. "I mean... Down here. In the dark. On your own."

"Right..." said Gwen. "And that's supposed to scare me into climbing the stairs, now, is it?"

"Something like that."

With Gwen stubbornly taking the lead, they climbed the stairs in almost complete darkness, each step marked out by the faintest trace of moonlight, until they reached the seventh floor.

"This is it," said Jack.

With his gun at his side, he led them out into a narrow corridor. The whole

The sky over the eastern edge of the valley was turning a pale shade of blue as they neared the limousine. Mr Croker pushed Toshiko into the car and the others climbed inside, with Mr Lime getting into the driver's seat. As the doors were closed, he turned the key in the ignition, but nothing happened.

"What is it?" asked Mr Glee. "Mr Lime... What's happening?"

"The car," he replied. "It won't start."

He'd no sooner spoken than the valley outside was filled with the cacophony of wailing sirens.

"What is it?" asked Kelly. "What's that noise?"

"The floodgates," hissed Mr Glee. "They're opening the floodgates."

He turned to Toshiko.

"The Book," he snarled. "You know how to use it. Get us out of here."

Mr Croker thrust the Book of Jahi into Toshiko's hands. It was so much heavier than she had expected.

All eyes were now upon her. She saw the guns in their hands and heard the sound of the sirens, and began desperately punching buttons and turning dials. She thought back to her notes, to what the symbols had meant, and to the video message left by Frank Jenkins.

It was as she worked on the Book and felt the thing hum with life that she saw, in one corner of her eye, a shape moving amid the trees. Glancing out too quickly for the others to notice, she saw Ianto, crouching down among the ferns and foxgloves.

The Book was beginning to glow now: an eerie purple light that spilled out between its keys. Mr Glee leaned forward, his dark eyes widening with anticipation. Toshiko looked up at him, and then at Kelly, and smiled back at them both.

"There," she said, triumphantly. "It works."

And with that she punched a final button and threw the Book at their feet. There was a sudden blinding flash of purple light which dazzled the others, and in one swift move Toshiko kicked open the door and rolled out of the car, landing in the road. She scrambled quickly to her feet and dived into the bushes at the roadside, where Ianto waited for her. He held out his hand to reveal four spark plugs.

"You're not the only technically minded one, you know," he said, smiling.

Toshiko turned to see the interior of the car lit up with that all-encompassing purple glow. It shone out through the windows in dazzling beams, nearly blinding her and Ianto, until it fully engulfed the limousine. The air around the car shimmered and shook, and even the sirens were drowned out by the sudden ear-splitting roar as a rift in space opened up around the vehicle and swallowed it whole. Then, as suddenly as it had begun, the noise and the light died down and the car was gone.

Ianto and Toshiko got to their feet and stepped down into the road, which was scorched black where the limousine had been.

"What did you do?" asked Ianto. "Where did you send them?"

"I'm not sure," said Toshiko, hesitantly.

With that there was another flash of light, this time in the valley below. It appeared on the rooftop of a tower block at the edges of the town, flaring brighter and brighter like a miniature star before fading to reveal the limousine.

"Oh," said Ianto. "That's not good."

"What do you mean?" asked Tosh.

"Well..." said Ianto, pointing to the far end of the valley.

Above the town, a great deluge of water had been unleashed, bearing down on the valley in separate rivers, which converged into a single unstoppable wave.

"Come on," said Ianto, "we need to get back to the car."

"What about Jack and Gwen?" said Tosh.

"We can't wait for them," Ianto replied. "We need to go. Now."

Toshiko nodded, and together they ran as fast as they could toward the gates and the SUV.

They were halfway there when the ferns at the roadside began to shake, and two muddy and bedraggled figures clambered awkwardly up onto the road itself.

"Short cut?" snapped Gwen, picking a twig from her hair, "That was your short cut?"

"Well," said Jack, "it worked, didn't it?"

Gwen turned to Ianto and Toshiko.

"Honestly," she said, "what I've just been through... I thought bungee jumping was bad."

She looked at Toshiko and smiled.

"You're okay!" she said. "But what about the others?"

Toshiko didn't reply. Instead she simply turned and looked down into the valley. Jack and Gwen followed her gaze until they saw the limousine parked on top of Bevan House.

"Tosh..." said Jack, "How did they get *there*?"

"The Book," said Toshiko, bashfully. "They told me to use the Book. So I did."

The grey waters of the reservoir now covered the lower levels of the town, rooftops vanishing beneath its tumultuous surface. Still, the waters came rushing down into the valley, swallowing everything in their wake until the tower block stood alone, slowly sinking under the waves.

"Come on," said Jack. "We can't do anything for them now."

They ran the short distance to the SUV and for a while they sat inside, watching as Cwmblaidd disappeared before their eyes. Soon enough even the tower block, the car, and its passengers were gone.

"So that's that," said Gwen. "The Book's exactly where Frank wanted it."

"Yeah," said Jack. "Probably for the best."

"All the research I could have done," said Toshiko. "All the things we could have learned..."

"Forget it, Tosh," said Jack, smiling at her in the rear-view mirror, "It's Cwmblaidd."

As they left the valley and joined the motorway, Jack called the Hub to tell Owen they were on their way home.

"All of you?" said Owen.

"All of us," said Jack.

"Thank God for that. I mean, I'd say you lot scared me half to death but, well... you know..."

Toshiko Sato dropped the notebook into her drawer, closed it, and turned the key. It was better that she kept it there, she had decided, where it was safe.

On the other side of the Hub, Owen was busy emailing their cover story to everyone from the water authorities to the local council and the police. The others were slumped in chairs, sitting in silence, except for Ianto, who busied himself making coffee. He brought Toshiko her cup last of all.

"You okay?" he asked.

Toshiko smiled.

"Yeah," she replied. "Glad to be home."

"Home?"

"Oh, you know... How's your head?"

"It'll mend," said Ianto, prodding the side of his head and wincing. "It's been a long day."

Toshiko nodded. She sipped her coffee and then placed the mug down on her desk before laughing softly.

"Something funny?" asked Ianto

"Just something that's been bothering me since we got back," she replied, with an awkward smile.

"What's that?"

Toshiko looked up at Ianto and her smile faded.

"Fish can swim," she said.

WHERE'S YOUR HEAD AT?

GARETH DAVID-LLOYD, OTHERWISE KNOWN AS COFFEE KING IANTO JONES, BELIEVES IN ALIENS, IS TERRIFIED OF SPIDERS AND LIKES DOING DANGEROUS THINGS! READ ON TO DISCOVER MORE OF HIS DEEPEST, DARKEST SECRETS...

What is the full name on your birth certificate?
"Gareth David Lloyd. David is my middle name, but I hyphenated it for my stage name when I joined Equity, because there's already another actor called Gareth Lloyd out there somewhere."

What is your nickname?
"My mates call me 'Gakloy' — kind of like J-Lo! You know how some people are so famous they just need one name? Well, that's mine! I think it just evolved from my mates saying 'Gareth Lloyd' over and over."

What is your earliest memory?
"Standing in my cot, being quite unhappy about the fact I couldn't get out. I must have been really young! After that, the next thing I remember going to hospital when I was 18-months old, after I pulled a kettle full of boiling water onto myself. That sticks in my mind for obvious reasons. I've still got the burn on my arm."

When was your first kiss?
"Without tongues? It was in a shed at the back of our house in Cardiff when I was eight years old. I was with my friend Felicity and I said, 'Let's kiss like they do on telly,' So we did! I had my first proper kiss a couple of years later, with a girl who was a bit more experienced than me. She just stuck her tongue down my throat, which I wasn't expecting at all! But I learned to like it eventually."

What was the last dream you had?
"I've been having a recurring dream about breaking up with my ex-girlfriend, which isn't very nice. I was quite hurtful to her, and I wish I hadn't been."

When was the last time you cried?
"Probably after that dream!"

Do you believe in aliens and/or the supernatural?
"Yeah. Too many weird things happen for me not to be a bit superstitious. Both me and my mum will think about things immediately before they happen, or mention someone just before we hear some bad news about them. As for aliens, I don't think I would be at all surprised to find out there was some degree of truth about government involvement in alien technology. I think all those conspiracy theories are fascinating." ▶

GARETH DAVID-LLOYD

What makes you happy?
"Intellectual, sincere music. In fact, it doesn't even have to be intellectual, as long as it's sincere. What else? Security, friendship... and adrenaline! I love to do things like snowboarding, and there are lots of other dangerous things I'd like to attempt. Sadly my contract doesn't allow me to do that at the moment!"

What scares you?
"Spiders! And confined spaces. I lost it a little bit when we were filming in the back of the truck for episode four [Meat]. There was just enough space for all of us and the camera, and it was very dark and very hot, and there wasn't much air. So I got a little bit claustrophobic and had to get out of there pretty quickly."

What drives you mad?
"Insincere music! Music that takes someone else's original idea and applies it to four or five guys who have to do exactly what they're told by their record producer. In fact, insincerity in general drives me mad. I don't like people who project an image of themselves that isn't real. I know it's a big element of the profession I'm in, but I don't like that at all."

When were you most embarrassed?
"I had a bit of an accident at my 26th birthday party, but I won't elaborate on that! Thinking about it, that was more embarrassing for other people anyway, because I was far too drunk to care. So, instead, I'll say my 70-year-old aunty walking in on me having sex when I was 17-years-old. She switched the light on, pulled back the covers and slapped my bare arse. That was really embarrassing."

"MY 70-YEAR-OLD AUNTY WALKED IN ON ME AND A GIRL WHEN I WAS 17. SHE PULLED BACK THE COVERS AND SLAPPED MY BARE ARSE."

What is your most treasured possession?
"My two dogs, Darcey and Maynard. They're named after the ballerina Darcey Bussell, and Maynard James Keenan, who's the singer with the band Tool. I adopted them both last year."

What are you reading at the moment?
"I'm re-reading The Dice Man by Luke Rhinehart, and Midnight's Children by Salman Rushdie at the moment. I tend to go back to a lot of books, because I'll pick up a big book and really enjoy it, but then realise that I didn't take it in as well as I should have!"

What's on your mp3 player?
"A lot of party music, acid jazz and underground funk. Then, for chilling out on my own, there's Portishead, Tool, Robert Johnson and a lot of other Delta blues singers. I'm really enjoying Down at the moment, too, which is Phil Anselmo's latest band."

What single item would you want with you on a desert island?
"A device that can turn human faeces into fuel."

What are you drinking?
"I like the organically produced lager you get in Sam Smith's pubs, and I always try to drink Brains SA if I see it as a guest ale when I'm not in Wales. Failing that, I'll have a glass of wine."

What is your favourite word?
"At the moment there's something about the word 'morose' I like. It's got a good sound to it."

What question do you wish you were asked in interviews?
"How do you stay so good looking! I bet John gets asked that all the time."

How do you stay so good looking?
"I think it's a natural gift."

What is the strangest place you've ever seen your image?
"It was on a cartoon porn website, actually! I didn't go looking for porn, I just put my own name into Google to see what came up! I've seen a few drawings of me that have been bordering on the inappropriate, but this was really bad!"

TORCH SONGS

MUSIC IS AN INTEGRAL PART OF EVERY TORCHWOOD EPISODE, FROM POP SONGS TO THE ORCHESTRAL SOUNDS OF COMPOSER BEN FOSTER

IT'S IMPOSSIBLE TO IMAGINE TORCHWOOD without the tunes, be they popular songs or original scores. Every episode features classic tracks and especially composed music by Ben Foster, and their insistent themes can stay with you for days afterwards. So here's our handy guide to the sounds of the show, with a rundown of the commercially available tracks featured in both series and which albums to find them on, plus over the page, we talk to Ben Foster himself about how he gives each episode its orchestral heart.

SERIES ONE

THE PIPETTES
We Are The Pipettes
Though never released as a single, this is the theme song of Brighton-based girl group The Pipettes, who echo the 1960s sound of producer Phil Spector.
Hear it in: **Everything Changes**
Find it on: **We Are The Pipettes (2006)**

THE KOOKS
She Moves In Her Own Way
The fifth single off The Kooks' debut album, this song reached number seven in the UK Singles Chart. It is rumoured to be about singer Katie Melua.
Hear it in: **Everything Changes**
Find it on: **Inside In/Inside Out (2006)**

SNOW PATROL
Spitting Games
No strangers to TV soundtracks, Snow Patrol can be heard in ER, Grey's Anatomy and Gavin And Stacey, with this song featuring twice in Torchwood!
Hear it in: **Everything Changes, Greeks Bearing Gifts**
Find it on: **Final Straw (2003)**

KAISER CHIEFS
Saturday Night
This track, from 2005's fourth best selling album, features the sound of a motorbike owned and 'played' by ex-Blur guitarist, Graham Coxon.
Hear it in: **Day One**
Find it on: **Employment (2005)**

GOLDFRAPP
Ooh La La
This lead single from Goldfrapp's third album reached number four in the UK charts, and was nominated for Best Dance Song at the Grammys in 2007.
Hear it in: **Day One**
Find it on: **Supernature (2005)**

TORCH SONGS

TRAVIS
Sing
This was the most played track on British radio in summer 2001, and was just as popular when it featured three times in Torchwood series one!
Hear it in: **Ghost Machine, Greeks Bearing Gifts, They Keep Killing Suzie**
Find it on: **The Invisible Band (2001)**

THE LIBERTINES
Can't Stand Me Now
The biggest hit for Pete Doherty's old band reached number two in the UK, and was later named one of the NME's '50 greatest indie anthems ever'.
Hear it in: **Ghost Machine**
Find it on: **The Libertines (2004)**

FEEDER
Feeling A Moment
This song, which reached number 13 in the UK singles chart, also features heavily in the BBC drama series Waterloo Road and in the film Goal II.
Hear it in: **Ghost Machine**
Find it on: **Pushing the Senses (2005)**

SNOW PATROL
Chocolate
Another song from Snow Patrol's highly acclaimed Final Straw, Chocolate also features in the 2006 movie The Last Kiss.
Hear it in: **Cyberwoman**
Find it on: **Final Straw (2003)**

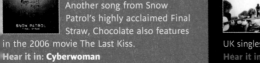

MOGWAI
We're No Here
Also featured in Miami Vice and Top Gear, the title originates from a mishearing of Celtic FC's chant 'Martin O'Neill' (the club's former manager).
Hear it in: **Cyberwoman**
Find it on: **Mr Beast (2006)**

HARD-FI
Better Do Better
The fifth and final single from Hard-Fi's debut album peaked at number 14 in the UK chart, and was the band's only single release during 2006.
Hear it in: **Small Worlds**
Find it on: **Stars of CCTV (2005)**

KAISER CHIEFS
Born To Be A Dancer
Named after the South African football club of the same name, the Kaiser Chiefs released four singles from their first LP, but this is an album track.
Hear it in: **Small Worlds**
Find it on: **Employment (2005)**

THE KOOKS
Ooh La
Not to be confused with Goldfrapp's Ooh La La, as heard in Day One, this track reached number 20 in the UK singles chart and also featured in American Idol.
Hear it in: **Small Worlds**
Find it on: **Inside In/Inside Out (2006)**

THE AUTOMATIC
Monster
This number three hit featured in the Doctor Who Confidential that followed the 2006 episode Fear Her. It has also appeared in ITV's Primeval.
Hear it in: **Countrycide**
Find it on: **Not Accepted Anywhere (2006)**

PLACEBO
Drag
Never released as a single, Drag featured on Placebo's fifth album, Meds. Music by the band can also be heard in Russell T Davies' drama Queer As Folk.
Hear it in: **Greeks Bearing Gifts**
Find it on: **Meds (2006)**

KT TUNSTALL
Suddenly I See
KT Tunstall won an Ivor Novello Award for this huge international hit, which also crops up on US dramas Grey's Anatomy, The Hills and Ugly Betty.
Hear it in: **Greeks Bearing Gifts**
Find it on: **Eye to the Telescope (2004)**

FUNERAL FOR A FRIEND
Red Is The New Black
Named after an Elton John track, these Welsh rockers are the first band ever to grace the cover of Kerrang! magazine before releasing an album.
Hear it in: **They Keep Killing Suzie** Find it on: **Casually Dressed And Deep in Conversation (2003)**

RIFF MANIPULATOR

100   100

50

WHEN THEY SHOOT, HE SCORES. TORCHWOOD COMPOSER **BEN FOSTER** ON HITTING ALL THE RIGHT NOTES…

How did you become composer for Torchwood?
"I'd been working as Murray Gold's orchestrator on Doctor Who since The Christmas Invasion, way back in 2005, and when Torchwood came round, Russell T Davies and Julie Gardner naturally asked Murray if he'd be interested in writing the music for that, too. He jumped at it, but said to me straight away that I might have to help him do a bit of composing, because of the workload involved with doing both shows. I was delighted, as I was when he first asked me to work on Doctor Who, because I've been a fan since I was a kid.

"As it turned out, Murray's deadlines started to pile up more and more, so he did the main theme, and two episodes [Everything Changes and Cyberwoman] for series one, then I did the rest. For series two, he did Kiss Kiss, Bang Bang, and a little bit in Exit Wounds, so out of 26 episodes, I've done 23. It was a lucky break, because although I've done lots of composing for TV, it was my first drama job, and that was what I really wanted to do. I was lucky that Murray is a very generous guy, and he's been very good at giving a lot of young folk chances in the industry."

What does being an orchestrator entail?
"Orchestration means taking a composer's cue and developing it into a finished piece. On Doctor Who, that usually means taking Murray's rough piano sketch and turning it into the orchestral sound that you hear on the show. It's great fun, because there are a lot of choices to make, and Murray will give me the freedom to experiment quite a lot. For Torchwood, I tend to do all my own orchestration, or to do it with my brother, Nick. I find that I can write stuff and develop it very quickly, so I don't really need anyone else to do it. I've got a piano that links up to the computer, so I can sit at the acoustic piano and play stuff in with the picture, and it tends to develop from there. It's great fun to do!"

How do you start composing for a new episode?
"I get sent the scripts early on, and I try to sit in on the tone meetings wherever possible, so I can get an idea of the direction a story might be going in. Then with something like From Out Of The Rain, I can immediately see that it's about a creepy ringmaster and a girl who likes water,

or with Adrift I can start to imagine scenes of the boat going across the water, which conjures up a particular sound in my mind.

"I tend to go with my first instincts in terms of coming up with a theme for something, because when I read something I tend to think that my first reaction is the most honest and the most natural. You could slave away for hours trying to come up with something else, but it probably wouldn't be any better. I never write stuff in full until I get the final edit, so until then I just play around with things and sketch them out on paper until the time is right.

"Whatever I come up with won't fit the picture exactly, but the essentials will be there, and I can speed it up or slow it down or whatever, working from that starting point."

How did the music change for series two?
"I think it's became a bit more emotional, because Murray started off with a very electronic approach in series one, with orchestra added to it later on. We talked in the break between series about where it should go from there, and my personal feeling was that it should be more orchestral, which I read as being more emotional at heart. Torchwood is about many different things, but at the crux of it, it's about life and death and the soul, and I can't paint those images without real musicians, because for me that's where the magic happens. It's like the difference between reading a script in a deadpan voice, and seeing it acted out in a way that really brings it to life.

"So with series two we used the BBC National Orchestra of Wales to record a load of themes, some of which I'd written for series one, so we had a strong library of material that I could use throughout the series. Then, later on, we did about six extra sessions with 12 string players in London, which gave us a really good, really big ▶

MIDDLE OF THE ROAD
Soley Soley
Most famous for Chirpy Chirpy Cheep Cheep, Middle Of The Road had two other big hits during the 1970s. This one make it to number two in the UK.
Hear it in: They Keep Killing Suzie
Find it on: The Best Of Middle Of The Road (2002)

LAMB
Górecki
Inspired by Henryk Górecki's third symphony, some of the lyrics to Górecki were used as dialogue for Nicole Kidman in the 2001 film Moulin Rouge.
Hear it in: They Keep Killing Suzie
Find it on: Lamb (1996)

Adrift

From Out Of The Rain

acoustic sound. It's still mixed together using electronics as well, but I think that using live musicians really gives it that edge."

Owen's theme is one of the most insistent and memorable from series two...
"Yeah... I found it the other day in episode three and I'd forgotten I'd put it in there! I think that shows how the music paves the way for things early on, almost subconsciously. It comes up at the end of episode five [Adam], when Tosh sees

music that's like a phoney ascension to heaven. I wrote that for They Keep Killing Suzie in series one, when Suzie is talking about the afterlife, and I re-recorded it with the orchestra for series two. I think Owen's theme is in every episode after that, except for Adrift. There's a particularly heavy version where it gets faster and faster at the end of Dead Man Walking, which is a version of the big theme from A Day In The Death. Then, in Exit Wounds, when Owen and Tosh are about to die, there's a mix-up of both their themes, too, which

ape the urban style of that a little bit. I actually alluded to the Gallifrey theme and the Doctor's theme in those episodes, too. Making those sorts of connections at three in the morning is what it's all about, really!"

How does composing for Torchwood differ from working on Doctor Who?
"Thematically you can't be quite so grand with Torchwood; you can't be so heart-on-your-sleeve. Murray and I talked about it very early on, and he

"I FOUND OWEN'S THEME IN EPISODE THREE [TO THE LAST MAN] THE OTHER DAY AND I'D FORGOTTEN I'D PUT IT THERE!"

the flowers, too, just to say that, okay, this is the Owen that wasn't, but there will be more with Owen and Tosh later on. I called it 'Minimal Theme One', because it's a really simple little scale. But it's useful if you can keep a theme simple, because it allows you to put it on top of almost anything. So I can play Owen's theme over Tosh's theme, or Jack's theme, transpose the key, move it around or slow it down very easily.

"Of course, Owen's theme really kicks off at the end of episode six [Reset], when he's been shot, and it's playing very slowly over a piece of

is much more effective than just writing a bit of generic sad music and slapping it on."

You also get to play with Murray Gold's theme for Martha in those episodes...
"Yes, and that was a great pleasure to do. It's always fun to reprise one of your own themes, but to be able to reference Doctor Who in that way is lovely, because it's like solving a massive join-the-dots puzzle in the back of your mind. Murray did some very hip, electric piano stuff for Martha when she was first in Doctor Who, so I tried to

said that it should be a bit more subtle, a little more clever almost, so you don't have to hammer stuff home so much. You have to be careful not to get into Doctor Who territory, where you really need to hold the audience all the time, though obviously that works perfectly for that show."

How do you decide when to use a pop song instead of an original piece of music?
"I'm actually not involved in those decisions at all. That's down to the producers and the director. I don't object to it: there are moments when rock

DAVID BOWIE
Starman
This song also features in the 2005 Doctor Who episode Aliens Of London, and drama Life On Mars.
Hear it in: Random Shoes
Find it on: Ziggy Stardust (1972)

ANTONY & THE JOHNSONS
Hope There's Someone
Taken from their 2005 Mercury Music Prize-winning album, this song just missed out on a Top 40 placing when it was released as a single in 2004.
Hear it in: Random Shoes, End of Days
Find it on: I Am A Bird Now (2005)

songs are used very well, like in To The Last Man, where the same song comes in at the beginning and the end [One Of These Mornings by Moby], but I think scored music can have a lot more to say most of the time.

"I also think using rock music makes things sound more American, and Torchwood isn't an American show; it has British sensibilities. They have very minimal budgets for composition in America, which is why they do it, so I have huge admiration for composers like Alf Clausen [on The Simpsons] and Michael Giacchino [Alias and Lost], who will defiantly use a full orchestra to achieve that very filmic sound. There's nothing worse than a very good show sounding a bit shabby because nobody spent any money on it."

What are your influences and inspirations?

"When I was young, I was really into things like The Prisoner, The Professionals, all the Gerry Anderson stuff, and obviously Doctor Who. Peter Howell [1970s/80s Doctor Who composer] was one of my music tutors at college, and I always used to point him out to impress my friends!

"In Torchwood, I don't think any of those shows are influencing me all that much, but I do think what they did was incredible and I do still love all that stuff. Looking at those old shows again, as I do every so often, you realise how fantastically written and cut to picture the music is, which was a lot harder to do in those days. Something like Laurie Johnson's music for The Avengers is a classic example of how to create a recurring character sound. He's one of my heroes as a TV composer, although he did films

as well. He was always incredibly efficient on a limited budget, and he gets as much out of it as possible, to create a really distinctive sound. It's really very clever, and I try to do that on Torchwood as well."

Do you have a favourite piece of music from your work on Torchwood?

"I'm very proud of the music for Out Of Time. That was actually a theme I wrote years ago, which I always wanted to use for something, and Out Of Time felt like the right time to use it. I also think the requiem for Jack when Gwen is watching over his body in End Of Days is very moving, because it's all done with real players. As I said before, it just wouldn't sound the same if it was me playing a synth string sound.

"In series two, Jonah's stuff in Adrift really moved me a lot, and the first time I watched it I actually cried. As a musician, the idea of that scream going on for so long is just a horrible nightmare. But I'm probably most pleased with Owen's theme, because we managed to weave it in so much, especially at the very end, which I thought worked very well. It sounds daft, but I genuinely feel a friendship with Owen and Tosh. Not with Burn and Naoko, but with the actual characters, simply because I spend so much time with them. When you write a cue for a chase scene, you honestly feel like you're the sixth member of Torchwood. It's the best feeling, it really is!"

The Avengers

TONY BENNETT
The Good Life
Despite being recorded by such luminaries as Frank Sinatra and Ray Charles, it was Tony Bennett's take on this song that hit the UK charts in 1963.
Hear it in: Out of Time
Find it on: I Wanna Be Around (1963)

HOT CHIP
Over and Over
This song from Hot Chip's Mercury Music Prize-nominated second album is also used as the theme tune to The Culture Show on BBC2.
Hear it in: Combat
Find it on: The Warning (2006)

CRAZY FROG
Crazy Frog
The Crazy Frog tune is, inexplicably, the most successful ringtone ever. Mixed with Harold Faltermeyer's 1985 hit Axel F, it went to number one in the UK.
Hear it in: Combat
Find it on: Crazy Frog Presents Crazy Hits (2005)

MUSE
Assassin
This release from Muse's fourth album reached number six in the UK Download Chart when it was released in that format alone in 2006.
Hear it in: Combat
Find it on: Black Holes And Revelations (2006)

THE STONE ROSES
Begging You
This was the last single released by Ian Brown and John Squire's band, and is loosely based on the Public Enemy track Fear Of A Black Planet.
Hear it in: End of Days
Find it on: Second Coming (1994)

RAY LAMONTAGNE
Trouble
The title track from LaMontagne's first album charted at number 25 in the UK, and can also be heard on the soundtrack of US drama Rescue Me.
Hear it in: Out of Time
Find it on: Trouble (2004)

GROOVE ARMADA
I See You Baby
Featuring Gram'ma Funk, this song was made popular by a Fatboy Slim remix, before featuring on the advertising campaign for the Renault Megane.
Hear it in: Out of Time
Find it on: Vertigo (1999)

TORCH SONGS

SERIES TWO

METHOD MAN
Release Yo'Delf
Method Man was the first member of the Wu-Tang Clan to go solo, and this single from his first album samples Gloria Gaynor's 1978 hit I Will Survive.
Hear it in: Kiss Kiss, Bang Bang
Find it on: Tical (1994)

BLUR
Song 2
Song 2 lasts for two minutes and two seconds, is the second track on the band's eponymous fifth album, and reached number two in the UK charts!
Hear it in: Kiss Kiss, Bang Bang
Find it on: Blur (1997)

ALABAMA 3
Mao Tse Tung Said
This song features a sample from cult leader Jim Jones. The band is most famous for performing Woke Up This Morning, the theme from The Sopranos.
Hear it in: Kiss Kiss, Bang Bang
Find it on: Exile On Coldharbour Lane (1997)

MUMM-RA
She's Got You High
Niall Buckler was just 14 when he formed Mumm-Ra, named after the villain from 1980s kids' show Thundercats. The band split in April last year.
Hear it in: To the Last Man
Find it on: These Things Move in Threes (2007)

MOBY
One Of These Mornings
Never released as a single, this song features in the US drama Without A Trace and in the 2006 movie version of Miami Vice.
Hear it in: To the Last Man
Find it on: 18 (2002)

THE BETA BAND
Squares
This song samples the 1968 hit Daydream by Wallace Collection, also used on the I Monster track Daydream In Blue in the same year.
Hear it in: To the Last Man
Find it on: Hot Shots II (2001)

MAGAZINE
I Love You You Big Dummy
Magazine covered this Captain Beefheart track as the B-side to 1978 single Give Me Everything. It now turns up on rarities collections.
Hear it in: Adam
Find it on: Scree (1991)

TRICKY
Christiansands
This track crops up in US drama 24 and in the movie Face/Off. Tricky himself appears in the 1997 film The Fifth Element.
Hear it in: Adam
Find it on: Pre-Millennium Tension (1996)

GORILLAZ
Feel Good Inc
Featuring De La Soul, Feel Good Inc reached number two in the UK charts, and was also heard in iPod commercials and BBC3 series Sinchronicity.
Hear it in: Reset
Find it on: Demon Days (2005)

ROOTS MANUVA
Awfully Deep
Roots Manuva's real name is Rodney Smith. His music also features in the movie Children Of Men and the Channel 4 drama Skins.
Hear it in: Dead Man Walking
Find it on: Awfully Deep (2005)

BATTLES
Atlas
An NME 'single of the week' this was the first Battles song to add vocals to their distinctive sound. It has also featured in US drama Nip/Tuck.
Hear it in: A Day in the Death
Find it on: Mirrored (2007)

SUPER FURRY ANIMALS
Fire In My Heart
Actor Rhys Ifans was briefly lead vocalist with this Welsh outfit before they hit the big time. This song reached number 25 in the UK.
Hear it in: Something Borrowed
Find it on: Guerrilla (1999)

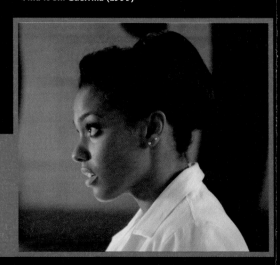

SUGABABES
Hole In The Head
Sugababes' third number one in the UK also topped the dance chart in the US, and was the band's first placing on the US Billboard Hot 100.
Hear it in: Something Borrowed
Find it on: Three (2003)

PAUL WELLER
You Do Something To Me
This solo song by the former Jam singer charted at number nine in the UK and features in the films The Bachelor and The Truth About Cats And Dogs.
Hear it in: Something Borrowed
Find it on: Stanley Road (1995)

SOFT CELL
Tainted Love
Soft Cell's take on this Gloria Jones classic appeared in the 2005 Doctor Who episode The End Of The World, The Office and Not Another Teen Movie.
Hear it in: Something Borrowed
Find it on: Non-stop Erotic Cabaret (1981)

SCISSOR SISTERS
Comfortably Numb
The Pink Floyd original was named one of Rolling Stone's '500 greatest songs of all time', and the band have expressed a liking for this disco cover version.
Hear it in: Something Borrowed
Find it on: Scissor Sisters (2004)

HARD-FI
Hard To Beat
Hard-Fi's first Top 10 single reached number nine in the UK charts when Gorillaz' Feel Good Inc (as heard in Reset) was at number eight.
Hear it in: Adrift
Find it on: Stars Of CCTV (2005)

HOT GOSSIP
I Lost My Heart To A Starship Trooper
This disco hit features soprano singer Sarah Brightman and charted at number six in the UK.
Hear it in: Exit Wounds
Find it on: Top Of The Pops 1978 (2007)

SCISSOR SISTERS
Filthy/Gorgeous
The only band to have two songs in the same episode, this track charted at number five in the UK, and was used in US drama Six Feet Under.
Hear it in: Something Borrowed
Find it on: Scissor Sisters (2004)

RICHARD HAWLEY
Serious
Richard Hawley played with The Longpigs and Pulp before finding solo success. he has also worked with Nancy Sinatra, Gwen Stefani and Elbow.
Hear it in: Adrift
Find it on: Lady's Bridge (2007)

KT TUNSTALL
Other Side of the World
The opening track from Tunstall's debut album and the second to feature in Torchwood, this was her first UK Top 20 hit, charting at number 13 in 2005.
Hear it in: Adrift
Find it on: Eye To The Telescope (2004)

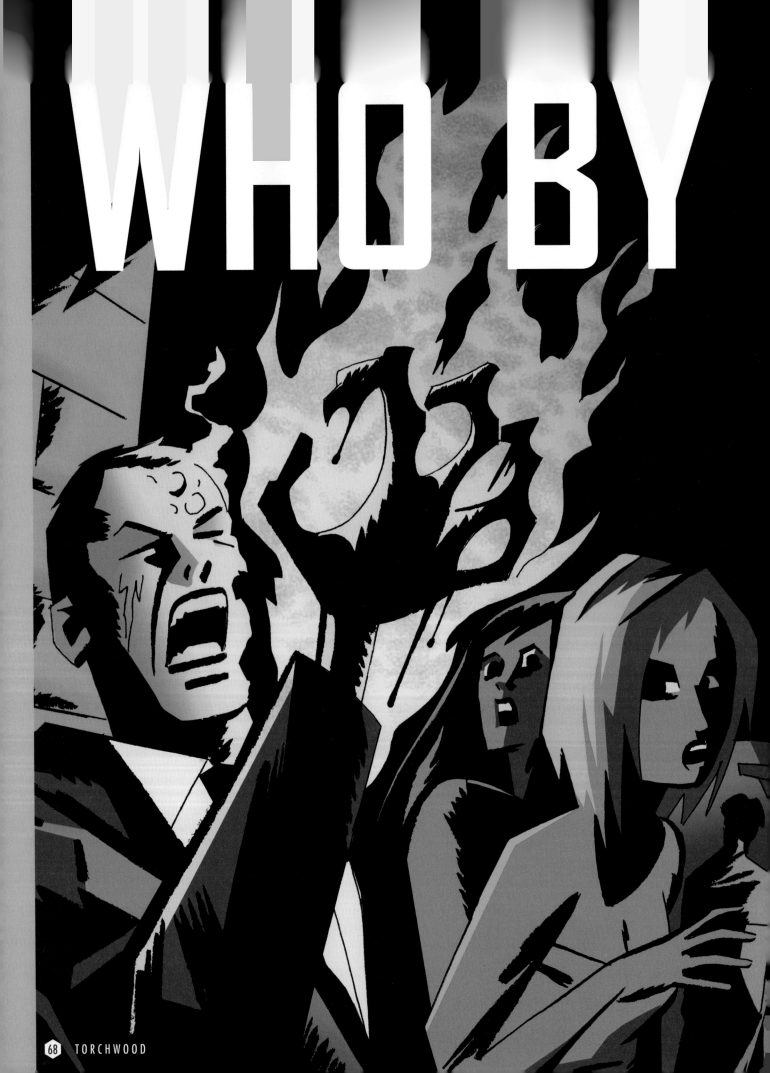

WHO BY

FIRE

A TORCHWOOD ADVENTURE BY ANDY LANE

ART BY ADRIAN SALMON

"This place stinks," growled Rick.

Craig turned to stare at his friend and colleague. Rick was in a black mood, hands shoved deep in his pockets and glowering at the mossy brick of the quayside a few feet away, his dark eyebrows drawn into a single line above his eyes.

Craig could feel the fractured breakbeats from the nightclub ship that was berthed alongside them thudding inside his chest, transmitted from the air and from the slabs that paved the pier. Each beat of his heart seemed to spawn two more beats in sympathy. His fingers twitched spasmodically in time with the music. The waiting was driving him crazy, but the club was one of the best on the Cardiff scene. There was always a queue, and the one that stretched ahead of Craig and Rick looked like it was going to take a good half-hour to negotiate.

Rick was hunched up: shoulders tense and face like thunder. It was as if he was already psyching himself up for a long and ultimately fruitless evening of shouting into girls' ears only to have them walk away when he tried to get a bit of face time with them; already writing the evening off before he'd paid his money to get in. As far as Craig was concerned there was always hope, but Rick's mind took a darker turn once he'd had a drink or two.

A couple of girls in the queue in front of them turned to check out Rick and Craig, then turned back dismissively, giggling to themselves at the suits and ties the two men were wearing. Craig had tried to persuade Rick that they should go home and get changed first, but as co-directors of Wilkins Advertising they'd been working late on a contract and Rick wanted to get trashed as soon as possible. The girls' clothes were garish and mismatched in the light spilling into the alley from the street, the skin on their shoulders corpse-white, but Craig knew that in a little while, when they were all inside and dancing, their clothes would be beautiful and their skin would glow with all the colours of the rainbow. And that would

last until the next morning, when – if he was lucky – he woke up next to one of them, only to find that the magic had worn off, leached away into the folds of the bedsheets, leaving only drab reality: a slack mouth, clothes piled on the floor, grainy skin smeared with old makeup, and the sound of snoring.

Assuming, that was, he could coax Rick down the gangplank.

"It stinks," Craig said heavily, "because people pee here. You peed here last week, when we came out, remember? You peed all over your shoes."

Rick's glower shifted away from the crumbling brickwork and towards his friend. "I wondered why they were wet when I got home. I thought it'd been raining."

"Rain doesn't smell like pee, and it isn't that colour."

Rick glanced at him. "How long have you lived in Cardiff?"

The line shuffled forward a few steps. Craig could see the bouncers at the head of the gangplank that led down to the ship, where the neon light from the sign above them made their shaven scalps glow like lightbulbs. Looking like they were powered from inside by alien technology, they checked people out, eyeballing them for attitude, making sure they could string a few coherent words together before letting them in. It's not that they were trying to stop trouble – trouble was pretty much guaranteed on a Wednesday night – it was more that they wanted the punters straight enough to spend some dosh on overpriced and watered-down drinks before the trouble actually started.

"I think tonight's going to be different," said Craig. He glanced along the queue at the light spilling out from the portholes, pulsating in time to the music. The two of them could do with a decent night out; they'd been pulling a load of midnight shifts recently, trying to get the company going. Fortunately they'd just secured a major contract, beating off several other companies, but it hadn't been easy getting the gig. The clients were more used to a slot during Coronation Street than viral advertising, webverts and ▶

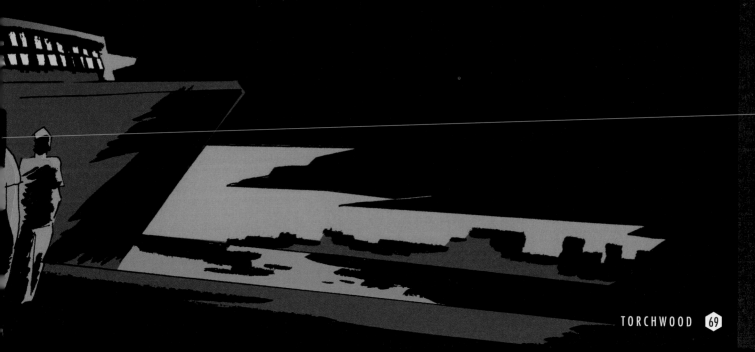

3G interactivity, and trying to get them to take on board the idea was like trying to explain brain surgery to a macaque monkey.

A cloud of smoke drifted past Craig, and he turned to give Rick a tongue-lashing. Rick kept promising he'd quit: smoking in front of clients was a no-no these days, and popping out every half hour for a quick fag got stale very quickly. There was no cigarette in his mouth, however, and his hands were empty. The smoke was rising from Craig himself; from the sleeve of his jacket. He ran his hand over it and found that it was hot. Roasting.

Rick frowned at Craig and looked as if he was about to say something, but he winced instead. The skin on his forehead was red, and it was blistering as Craig watched. The sweat suddenly pouring down his face was turning Rick's collar into a damp rag. The girls in front of them had noticed that something was wrong, and were backing away. The bouncers were moving towards them, menacingly.

Craig's hand felt hot. He raised it in front of his face and watched, uncomprehendingly, as it burst into flame.

The last thing he ever saw was the flesh melt and trickle away, leaving the bones of his fingers sticking up, burning and cracking as he watched.

the Hub. "Nobody to do autopsies, nobody who can program a computer worth a damn – we're still operating with our hands tied behind our backs here."

"You could always advertise in the local paper," Ianto ventured. "Wanted: social misfits with low self-esteem to die in secret and bizarre ways while saving the world. Free pizza. No holidays."

"Not helping," Jack said quietly. "Not helping at all."

"Not trying to," Ianto muttered, more to himself than anyone.

"It's not the first time it's happened," Gwen interjected, more to interrupt the subtle bickering that indicated a recent Jack and Ianto row than for any other reason. "I've got three other deaths by fire on record over the past month."

"Why didn't we spot anything odd before?" Jack asked. "Isn't that supposed to be our job?"

"One of them was listed as an unexplained vehicle fire, one as a house fire caused by an electrical short circuit and one as a suicide. This is the first one to happen in public. Do you know how many people die in Cardiff every week? I mean the ones that have nothing to do with aliens. We can't investigate them all, no matter how many of us there are."

weeks – literally. A lot of new business has suddenly hit them."

"You think they're weeding out the competition with some kind of alien technology? Isn't that a bit, well, obvious?"

"They work in advertising," Jack replied dryly. "Subtlety is not their strong suit." He tapped the earpiece that was discreetly tucked away beneath his hairline. "Ianto, can you hear me?"

"Yes sir," Ianto's voice said tinnily in their ears. "This thing is so sensitive I can hear the sound of your teeth grinding together and Gwen's indigestion. Which she should get treatment for, by the way."

"Okay. Anything else worth mentioning come in on the police computer?"

"I took some time to read through the witness statements from the bouncers and the other people outside the nightclub. They all mentioned seeing smoke rising from the shoulders and heads of the two victims. One girl said that the fire started in one man's hair, and the other man's hand when he raised it in front of his face. And the bits of the bodies that were left more or less unscathed were their feet and lower legs."

"And this means..?"

"That in the absence of any other information,

"LIKE AN ENERGY WEAPON OF SOME KIND?" GWEN ASKED. "YES I WOULD, ACTUALLY," SAID IANTO. "I'M BEGINNING TO THINK THAT PTERODACTYL DOESN'T LIKE ME VERY MUCH."

And the last thing he felt was incredible, intense heat as his whole body caught fire and burned, burned like the sun.

"No sign of any accelerants, according to the police report," Gwen called up to Captain Jack Harkness, who was in the hot house on the upper level of the Hub. "And no indications of what caused the fire in the first place. It's a puzzle."

"Crosswords are a puzzle," Ianto remonstrated from the terminal next to hers. "The deaths of innocent people are more usually called tragedies."

"And a possible indicator of alien activity, in this case," Jack called back. "Can we do our own autopsy? Find something they missed?"

"No," Gwen replied, "for two reasons. Firstly, what's left of the bodies would just about fit into a Starbucks mug and still leave room for milk, and secondly, even if they were intact, I can't even carve a lamb joint without turning half the meat into shreds. Autopsies are not part of my skill set, Jack. I'm getting all this from the police reports."

Jack emerged from the flora of the hot house and stood on the gantry, looking down into

"So what connects these other deaths to our disco inferno?"

"The lack of any obvious cause... And the fact that all the victims were senior advertising executives."

"Someone's trying to wipe out advertising executives?" Ianto asked. "Those Currys adverts must have made it through the Rift."

Jack moved down the stairs with his usual grace and economy of movement. "Gwen, check all the advertising companies in the Cardiff area."

"Looking to see how many have lost a senior executive recently?"

"No," he said grimly. "Looking to see which one hasn't."

Southerland House was a prestigious tower in green glass and purple neon-lit scaffolding that sat in the centre of Cardiff's properous business district.

"They must be doing well for themselves," Gwen said, staring up at the glowing lines that silhouetted the building against the night sky, like something from an anime cartoon.

"Better now," said Jack. "Most of their competition has melted away in the past few

whatever caused them to burst into flames happened from above."

"Like an energy weapon of some kind?" Gwen asked.

"Yes, I would actually," Ianto's voice said in their earpieces. "I'm feeling a little edgy, here by myself. I'm beginning to think that pterodactyl doesn't like me very much."

"No," she said patiently, "I meant, was that what caused them to burst into flames?"

"Oh." Ianto paused. "I see. Yes, I think it probably was. Best guess would be some kind of microwave projector, but there were no high buildings around where someone could have fired from. They were standing on the quayside, waiting to go into that new nightclub that's moored there."

"What, the ship?" Gwen asked. "Rhys keeps telling me he's going to take me there."

"I keep hoping someone will take me," Ianto said pointedly.

"Children, concentrate!" Jack chastised. "Gossip later; save the world now. So we've got a possible energy beam from above, when there is nothing above. Ianto, check the space activity

logs for the times the deaths occurred. See if there were any objects in orbit overhead at the time."

"Okay..." said Ianto, who was still getting to grips with the intricacies of Tosh's software. "I think I've got it. There's an icon that looks like a little planet... Ah! Interesting!"

"What is?"

"If I understand this program correctly, there's a satellite orbiting the Earth that's only been there for a few weeks. And it was above Cardiff every time there was a suspicious, fiery death."

"Satellite or spaceship?" Jack came back.

"Satellite," Ianto replied. "Or a spacecraft for very tiny aliens. Which isn't beyond the realms of possibility, I suppose."

"If it was a satellite, when was it launched?" Gwen asked.

"That's interesting, too," Ianto replied. "It wasn't. Apparently, it just appeared in orbit one day. And it's not technically in orbit: it's at one of the Lagrange points of gravitational equilibrium between the Earth and the moon. If that means anything. Which it doesn't to me."

"Shouldn't UNIT have spotted a new satellite?" Gwen asked Jack.

"There's a lot of things UNIT should do, but don't," Jack said grimly. "And a lot of things they do that they probably shouldn't. That's one of the reasons we exist." He raised his voice slightly. "Good work, Ianto. We're going into the Southerland Building. If we're not out in two hours..."

"Then what?" Ianto asked as Jack paused for a moment.

"Then you'll have to go to that floating nightclub by yourself," he said.

Lights were on in some of the offices, and there was a security guard at the front desk, but Jack and Gwen managed to get into the building and up to a deserted floor by the simple expedient of claiming to have an appointment and keeping the guard busy in conversation while Ianto hacked into the company's computer from the Hub and fed their details in. The guard took their pictures with a webcam and printed security passes for them to wear. He didn't seem to be bothered that someone would have an appointment at three o'clock in the morning. Perhaps, Gwen speculated, that was standard procedure in the advertising industry.

Jack had a small scanner in his hand, and was checking the display as he walked along the pastel-carpeted corridors.

"What have you got?" Gwen asked.

"Some kind of signal," he said. "Transmitted from somewhere nearby, and highly directional. Probably aimed at that satellite. I can't detect anything coming back down, though. It's purely one-way traffic." He led the way to a door with a sign on it saying 'Peter Southerland – Creative Director'. He twisted the doorknob and pushed the door open without knocking. Gwen heard the splintering sound of a breaking lock as he turned the doorknob.

"Strong," she said, admiringly.

"Bad workmanship," he replied, but he was smirking. ▶

The room was empty, but Gwen's attention was dragged straight away to the device that sat over to one side of the office. It looked a little as if someone had played a blowtorch over a pile of garden tools, but there was an obvious screen and some glowing buttons. Jack went straight to it.

"It's an alien control device and transmitter," he said. "It's humming with Rift radiation, so I'd guess it came through recently. Either this Southerland guy got lucky and found it, or he sought it out at some underworld auction. As soon as he activated it, it communicated with that satellite up there, which followed the signal through hyperspace to get to Earth. That's why it seemed to appear out of nowhere. My guess is that it's an unmanned weapons platform of some kind, and Southerland is getting trigger happy to eradicate his competition. How petty and venal you people can be."

"Hey, don't tar me with that brush!" Gwen protested. "I've never even written a poison-pen letter, let alone fried anyone with a outer-space-based flame thrower!"

"More like a heat ray," Jack corrected. He crossed to the desk and picked up something small, but of a similar design to the device in the corner. "Remote control," he added grimly, punching at the controls. "Makes it almost too easy."

Gwen glanced at the larger device in the corner. "How's he been deflecting questions about it?" she wondered. "I mean, it's hardly discreet."

"I tell people it's a modern art sculpture," said a voice. "Nobody's called my bluff just yet, but then, nobody here really knows that much about modern art."

Gwen spun round. The man standing in the doorway was thin, and wore a black suit with a round, Indian-style collar. His hair was teased up into a quiff, and his face was aquiline and hard-edged.

"Mr Southerland, I presume?" said Captain Jack.

"Intruders, I presume," Southerland replied. "And ones that know far more than they should."

A whooping alarm sounded in the corridor outside.

"Time to leave," Jack said to Gwen. He moved around the side of the desk, still holding the remote control. Southerland took two steps towards him and snatched it from his hand. Jack stared at him for a moment, and then strode towards the doorway.

"You won't get far," Southerland said, waving the remote control at him. "I can't afford to let you leave."

"Try to stop us," Jack said, and pulled Gwen through the doorway.

He turned to the right as they exited and tugged her along the corridor towards the lifts.

"What are we doing?" she asked. "Is there a plan, or are we just running away?"

"There's a plan," he replied. "There's always a plan. Of course, sometimes that plan does involve running away as well. The two are not mutually exclusive. I learned that from a friend a long time ago."

The lift was still on their floor, where they, or Southerland, had left it. As the door slid shut behind them Jack pressed the button for the top floor.

"Er, the exit's on the ground floor, Jack," said Gwen.

"We're not exiting," Jack replied. "We're fighting back."

The lift took them to the top floor, and a maintenance stairway led to a door which gave access to the roof. Cold winds whipped across the weatherproofed exterior, where extractor fans for the air conditioning were scattered round like metal mushrooms.

Jack led Gwen across the roof to a spot positioned between two of the mushrooms, then stopped. "Here, I think," he said, looking around.

Before Gwen could say anything, the door to the stairwell flew open and Peter Southerland stepped out onto the roof, the remote control for the weapons platform held in his left hand.

"Tactical mistake," he said, "heading upwards. You thought I'd head down? Now you've nowhere to go, and you're entirely at the mercy of my Fire from Heaven!"

"Fire from Heaven?" said Jack? "That's just cheesy. I'm not surprised you needed to get rid of the competition."

Southerland smiled, and raised the remote control. "The great thing about this system," he said, "is that I don't even have to type in coordinates. I just point this thing at you, and it does the rest for me." He held the remote control out and pressed something. A light flashed briefly on the front. "Job done. Goodbye."

"If you get burned to ash," Gwen whispered to him, "can you survive? I mean, is that the plan? I get burned to a crisp, but you survive and take him out?"

"No," he said, "that's not the plan."

Gwen looked up, waiting for the sudden heat of the weapon above to incinerate them both. "Then what *is* the plan?"

Jack gently pushed Gwen to one side. She took two steps and stopped. He took two steps in the opposite direction.

"The plan," he said, "depends on the fact that microwaves travel at the speed of light, and light takes around 16 seconds to travel between one of the Lagrangian points of gravitational stability and the surface of the Earth. Which means Southerland's 'Fire from Heaven' should be arriving..." He consulted his watch. "Right around now."

Gwen looked up again, and saw the raincloud above her glow in a perfect cylinder as something burned its way through the air itself. The tarmac of the roof bubbled between her and Jack, then melted way to form a perfect hole a metre wide. She felt a wave of heat pass her by.

"Did I mention," Jack called conversationally to Southerland, "that I boosted the power levels when I picked up your remote control? Normally that microwave weapon would just have enough power to incinerate a human being, but I decided to knock it up a bit. Just for the hell of it. And, of course, to ensure that the beam would destroy the alien transmitter, eight storeys below where we're currently standing."

The wave of heat that had swept past Gwen vanished. The tarmac around the hole still bubbled, but Gwen could see it congealing as she watched. She glanced into the fissure and saw how it sliced through the building, storey after storey. There were small fires breaking out below.

"What now?" she asked Jack across the fissure. "The device is destroyed and the remote control is useless. So I guess the weapons platform just stays there, useless, too."

"Now," said Jack, as Southerland backed towards the stairway, "you stop me throwing him off the roof. Just for the hell of it."

THE FALL GUY

DAREDEVIL PERFORMER **CURTIS RIVERS** DROPS IN TO TELL US WHY BEING CAPTAIN JACK'S STUNT DOUBLE IS LIKE FALLING OFF A LOG. IF THE LOG IS SUSPENDED OVER 100 FEET IN THE AIR…

IT'S GONE MIDNIGHT WHEN A BODY PLUMMETS from the roof of the British Gas building in central Cardiff. It's not a dummy, and it's not a greenscreen trick. Dressed in the distinctive outfit of Captain Jack Harkness, which billows wide as he falls, this is Curtis Rivers, professional action man and long-time stunt double for John Barrowman.

At ground level, assistant directors and producers watch the descent on a large monitor, while curious members of the public forgo their beds out of curiosity. Tonight's stunt will eventually form the centrepiece of Torchwood's series two opener, Kiss Kiss, Bang Bang, as Captain John Hart pushes Captain Jack to his latest spectacular death. Unbeknown to the watching public, John Barrowman and James Marsters themselves are on the roof of the 11-storey building, preparing to film their scenes, but for now all eyes are on Curtis.

To achieve the fall safely and effectively, a huge mobile crane has been squeezed into the built-up street, its telescopic boom reaching past the top floor of the office block and high into the night sky. At one end of the crane's wire rope, Curtis is attached by a harness that allows him to move his arms and legs freely. At the other end, a powerful 4x4 serves as the counterweight, hoisting Curtis into the air by reversing along the traffic-free street, before exactly the right amount of rope is released for his drop.

He lands squarely in an oversized air cushion (accurately described by associate producer Sophie Fante as "a lovely big bouncy castle"), and is met by stunt coordinator Tom Lucy, who has worked closely with the production team to achieve this and every other stunt on the show. A shout goes round that Curtis is okay, followed by an audible exhalation of relief from the entire crew. The shot is in the can, and Curtis has survived another of Captain Jack's deaths. As he slips out of Jack's hefty coat and the harness beneath, Curtis has only one word to describe the experience. "Exhilarating!" he says.

A few months later, we caught up with Curtis once again, now with his feet firmly on the ground, and with some time to discuss his work as the unknown face of one of TV's most recognisable heroes. One question presents itself as an obvious starting point: what on Earth makes somebody think, "I want to become a stuntman"?
"I really can't remember what the trigger was, but I can remember writing to the BBC when I was eight years old to find out how I could do it!" he says. "That led to me getting a list of the required qualifications from The British Actors Equity Association. To become a member of their prestigious Stunt Register you have to be an actor [Curtis graduated from the New Era Academy of Speech and Drama in 1994], and be highly experienced in judo, fencing, horse riding, trampolining, swimming, springboard and rescue diving, parachuting, gliding and personal survival! That only gets you a probationary membership, after which you have to do another five-year apprenticeship, always adding new disciplines."

So, as if that wasn't enough, what other disciplines have you mastered?
"My current skills include fast precision driving, ramp jumps and crashes, high falls into water or airbags, car knockdowns, full body fire burns, harness and wire work, fight scenes including martial arts and weapons, stair falls, and swordfights using sabres, epées, foil and broadswords! I'm also a qualified offshore rescue diver and ASA swimming coach, and I hold the Guinness World Record for the highest bungee jump [15,200ft] ▶

Getting grubbied up by the costume team.

and the longest parachute flight [30,000ft]. I've used a lot of those skills on Torchwood, but there are still plenty of things up my sleeve that we've yet to use for Captain Jack."

Is it scary work, or have you overcome your fears after doing it for so long?
"Oh, I still get nervous. I think it's quite healthy to feel fear, and I'd be very concerned if I didn't, because the adrenaline helps to sharpen the mind and enhance your reaction time. It's not so much the fear of injury, because we prepare and test everything so thoroughly. I'd liken it more to the adrenaline any actor might feel before going on stage for a performance. And, just like that analogy, the moment the cameras roll, there's no fear at all: it's just 100 percent concentration."

Is there a big difference between Torchwood and movies you've worked on, such as Hot Fuzz and The Da Vinci Code?
"More than you might imagine, actually! The main difference is in the budget of course, but there are lots of ways to shoot a stunt, so it is possible to achieve a similar result on a big budget, or for a fraction of the cost, so hopefully people don't notice the difference so much. A huge explosion in a movie, that blows stunt performers through third floor windows in a fireball, might become a simulated blast using compressed air and cork board in Torchwood, blowing the stunt performers to the floor! Our stunt coordinator Tom Lucy does a great job of translating the action from script to screen in a believable way."

Do you ever argue with John Barrowman over who gets to do Captain Jack's stunts?
"Well, I'm sure John will tell you how much he likes to do all his own stunts, but there's a very definite line in TV and film stuntwork, which simply can't be crossed. Even if an actor is a highly skilled physical performer, who is confident in his ability to do the stunt, we just can't allow that risk. As a general rule

Making a splash as Captain Jack gets shot at the start of Exit Wounds.

"I THINK IT'S QUITE HEALTHY TO FEEL FEAR. I'D BE VERY CONCERNED IF I DIDN'T."

of thumb, if an actor does it, it's not a stunt. Some actors will come close to the line, but the stunt coordinator is always there to remind them not to even think about crossing it!"

Is it important you resemble the person you're doubling, or is that all achieved with makeup?
"It's important that John and I have a similar build, but I'd be flattered if someone said I looked like him! I always study the person I'm doubling very closely when they're in character, and even when they're off set, to see how they move, and I watch the rehearsal so I can mimic the actor's reaction when we overlap, for a seamless switch.

"My hair is generally shorter than John's, so I do have a wig standing by, but I grew my hair for series two of Torchwood, so I didn't have to spend so much time in the makeup chair. Now I just turn up for work and put the Captain Jack outfit on, and I'm good to go!"

What's the most challenging stunt you've had to perform on Torchwood?
"It's difficult to pinpoint a particular stunt, but the ones that look easy are often the most tricky to do! One that does stand out in my mind from season one, though, is the shot of Jack standing right on the edge of that 240ft building [see picture]. It was a very surreal experience for me, because I was only attached to the building by a thin wire, which was secured a few storeys below. If I'd fallen, I'd have had a nasty spill, though not a fatal one. The director was in a helicopter, talking to me via an earpiece. He told me to look up above the horizon, so I had 240ft of fresh air below me, and no visual reference point at all! There was nothing to lean on either, so the wind made me sway back and forth. I was very pleased with the shots, but I was happy when I returned to the ground in a lift!

"Then, very different from that, being pushed into the grave by Gray in Exit Wounds was tricky, even though it looks like a simple stunt. The grave was too small to 'push off' into, and it was ▶

COOPER TROOPER

WHENEVER GWEN COOPER TAKES A TUMBLE OR A PUNCH, EVE MYLES STANDS ASIDE AND STUNT PERFORMER **JO McLAREN** STEPS IN...

What's it like to be Eve Myles' stunt double?
"It's great, and Eve is great, too. After I've done a stunt, she'll come up to me and say, 'That was amazing, thanks for making me look good!' She's very physical, but also very professional, so she steps back whenever Tom Lucy the stunt coordinator says so. I'm sure if she was allowed she'd be up for doing more. She's lovely and an absolute scream."

Have you doubled for actors other than Eve in the show?
"I also doubled for Indira Varma [Suzie Costello] in the first series, and for Colette Brown when she jumped through the window [as Carrie in Something Borrowed]. That was probably one of my favourite stunts on Torchwood. But I've mainly doubled for Eve in fight sequences and things, and I've done a little bit of stunt driving."

How did you first get into stunt work?
"I did a lot of sword fighting and martial arts and stuff at drama school, and I rode horses, so I had a fairly physical background. Then one of my first acting jobs was on [JC Wilsher's police drama] Between The Lines, where there were

Something Borrowed

a lot of stunts and fight scenes going on. When I saw what the stunt guys were doing, I thought it looked like my cup of tea. So I started my training while I was still at drama school, and got my qualifications that way. You've got to have acting skills, even if you're being blown up or falling off something!"

Do you get much opportunity to use those skills in Torchwood?
"I do sometimes. I was one of Ianto's victims when he thought he was a serial killer in Adam. Gareth [David-Lloyd] played a great murderer! It was pretty gruesome, and it was a very cold, wet night with the rain effects coming down and me freezing in a little short skirt! But it was good fun to do a bit of acting. I like playing the little parts, then following it through with the stunts. It's great."

What stunts would you like to see Gwen doing in the future?
"I'd like her to do a bit of aerial work, running across the rooftops, followed by a big fall on a descender, followed by a big fight! Then her legs would catch fire!"

Top to bottom: Secured in a harness and suspended from a crane, stunt performer Crispin Layfield hangs around with James Marsters to film Captain John's first appearance in Kiss Kiss, Bang Bang.

"I HAD 240 FEET OF FRESH AIR BELOW ME, AND NO REFERENCE POINT!"

too shallow to flip over to my back correctly. We pulled it off safely by adapting the start position so I could begin away from the edge, and we lined the bottom with a layer of boxes, known as a box rig, to lessen the impact when I landed on my shoulders. Had I got that one wrong I'd have landed on my head and broken my neck, which is why we take such stringent safety precautions."

True to its name, Kiss Kiss, Bang Bang must have been a packed episode for you...
"It was! We had the barroom brawl, which saw me somersaulting through a Japanese screen and bursting through a window with James Marsters' stunt double; three of us simulated the Rift explosion by simultaneously diving off trampettes while air mortars were triggered behind us; and I was thrown backwards in a harness off the top of the 140ft British Gas building in Cardiff! My colleague Crispin Layfield also did a 60ft drop from the same car park used for the Rift explosion, for the scene where Captain John first appears [see left]. So there were a lot of stunts in that episode, yes!"

How involved are you in the stunt driving sequences?
"Oh, I've spent many nights throwing that SUV around Cardiff! I've hurtled round corners, skidded and screeched to a halt, sped after aliens and rushed to and from the Hub many times! In reality, the SUV is a bit of a nightmare to drive, because it not only has these anti-skid and anti-wheelspin devices built in, but it also has false wing mirrors and no rear window to see out of when reversing! In one shot, I had to miss a turning that a Weevil had run down, slam on the brakes, then reverse back quickly to hit the exact mark for the camera. Imagine what it's like reversing a big SUV in the dark, at speed, in the rain, with zero visibility behind you! You have to use a lamppost or some other landmark as a marker for when to stop. It's extremely difficult. I'm hoping Captain Jack destroys the SUV in the next series! I'd definitely be up for rolling it, given the opportunity!"

Is there any particular stunt that you'd love to do in Torchwood one day?
"I'd like to see Captain Jack's unique immortality used for some more unusual stunt sequences.

Not John Barrowman

ACTION PLANNER

TORCHWOOD STUNT COORDINATOR **TOM LUCY** IS ALWAYS ON HAND TO MAKE SURE NONE OF HIS PERFORMERS BREAK A LEG...

Take fire, for example: imagine if an alien were to tip blazing oil all over him! Jack would go up into a full blaze, but he'd grit his teeth and keep on running until he captured the alien! Only then would he stop to put himself out. Usually when a man catches fire on TV, he waves his arms around and slumps to the floor, but in Torchwood you could have amazing scenes of him sprinting through the streets of Cardiff! I've been set on fire before, and it would be totally safe to film."

So what advice would you give to budding stunt men and women?

"The first bit of advice I'd give anyone thinking about becoming a stunt performer is, 'Stop thinking about becoming a stunt performer!' It takes many, many years of dedicated hard graft to become qualified, and many more years of difficult slog to master the skills on set. Plus, at the end of all that, there's no guarantee that you'll actually get work! Like all kinds of actors, a far larger proportion of stunt performers are 'resting' than working at any one time.

"That said, if knowing all that still doesn't put you off, you should get into acting first, get an Equity card, then develop your skills, like martial arts, swimming, climbing and driving, to the standards set by the Joint Industry Stunt Committee [JISC] Register. Those standards are updated all the time, so anyone training has to keep checking their skills are current."

Finally, is Torchwood really worth taking so much punishment for?

"It really is, yes! I enjoy every minute of it. There's a real family atmosphere, and everyone is really down to earth. I've also had a schoolboy crush on Eve Myles since series one, so going to work is an extremely pleasant experience!" ▣

What does your job as stunt coordinator on Torchwood entail?

"I get the script and I go through it with the director to decide what stunts we can afford, and how we can do them. Then I talk through the requirements with whoever else needs to be involved, whether it's the props department or the location manager or even the costume designer. We'll do a recce of the location and plan everything out with the performers and the crew, and we'll do plenty of rehearsals to make sure everything's safe and everyone knows what's going on."

Do you ever disagree with the director about how to film a particular stunt?

"No, not on Torchwood, anyway. Sometimes a director's vision might be slightly different from what you think is feasible, but you say, 'Well, we can't do that, but I can give you this to achieve a similar shot. Generally they'll be very happy with that."

Do you have to talk the actors out of doing their own stunts?

"Sometimes. Some of the young guys are very able and want to jump around, but some of the others are very happy to have a stunt double. Most of the action tends to feature John, but Gareth [David-Lloyd] always gets really into it whenever he has a chance to do some stunts, and James Marsters told me he enjoyed having a fair bit to do. We tried to use him and John as much as possible in the barroom fight, so we could get lots of close-ups on their faces."

Were you a stunt man before becoming stunt coordinator on Torchwood?

"I was, and I never actually set out to be a stunt coordinator. It was just a natural progression from being a stunt man. Performing was always my first love, but these days I'm so busy that I only do a stunt myself if it's something I really want to do."

What's the most challenging part of your job?

"Very high falls can be tricky, and anything with cars, purely because of the logistics involved in using roads and real vehicles, which aren't specially designed props. Fire stunts can be

Tom puts Gareth David-Lloyd through his paces on the set of Meat.

quite challenging for a lot of people, too, though I don't mind fire, because I started out as a stunt coordinator on London's Burning!"

Do you liaise with the effects team a lot?

"I do, and we work together very well. I've known the Any Effects boys since we all worked on London's Burning, years ago, so now I trust them, and they trust me about how close we can get to the explosions. So in something like Sleeper, where the front of that building blows up in the city centre, we were able to get people right there in front of it. An explosion on its own does look great, but it's not until you start sticking people into it that you understand and relate to the jeopardy, so I was very pleased with how that turned out."

How has stunt work changed since you began your career?

"In the old days, you could throw stunt people off a building, but if you asked them to do any sort of acting, they would just fall apart. But the modern day stunt person is more of an 'action actor', who is more than happy to go in, do the action and do dialogue, too. So people like Derek Lea [who played a paramedic in Sleeper] and Jo McLaren [see page 51] are very talented actors, whom you can film up close and personal, rather than always hiding the faces when the action starts."

OWEN

GWEN

JACK

Torchv

TOSH

IANTO

Choose life. Choose a job. Choose risking your life
to save humanity from the perils of the 21st Century.
But which member of the team would you choose to be?
Turn the page to find out now!

vood

WHICH MEMBER OF THE TEAM ARE YOU? ▶

A re you more Captain Jack than Constable Cooper? Or perhaps you're a little more Harper than Harkness? We all have different priorities in life, and different personality traits that make us who we are. In extreme circumstances, such as those faced by the Torchwood team every day, those traits can be magnified tenfold. So why not take our test and see which member of the team you would most resemble in a fix? Make a note of your answers as you go, and don't forget, it's just for fun!

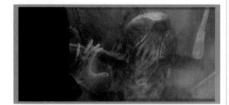

Q1 What's your take on extraterrestrial life?
a) Just another day at the office.
b) Frightening, fascinating, and a whole lot of fun.
c) It's all right as long as you don't fall in love with it.
d) I prefer it locked up, strapped down, and out like a light.
e) It's easier to understand than human life.

Q2 You come across a Weevil on your way home from a night out. Do you...
a) Invite it back to yours for a nightcap and a cuddle.
b) Pull out your gun and phone your other half to tell them it's going to be a late one.
c) Stay in the shadows and hope you blend into the night.
d) Challenge it to a cage fight.
e) A night out? Didn't I have any work to do?

Q3 Which alien species do you have most in common with?
d) Weevils
e) The Butterfly People of Arcateen 5
a) Blowfish
b) I prefer humans
c) Cybermen

Q4 How would you describe yourself in a lonely hearts column?
a) Hot, horny and out of this world!
b) Friendly and feisty, with own set of handcuffs!
c) Sophisticated, suave type who'll swing both ways.
d) Cocky, confident and crafty with my hands.
e) Shy, sexy, and scarily scientific.

Q5 What do you enjoy doing in your free time?
a) Travelling, meeting new people, just surviving...
b) Hanging out with my partner, having a laugh, target practice.
c) Ironing, drinking coffee, playing some naked hide-and-seek.
d) Eating, drinking, loving.
e) Reading, surfing the internet, sudoku.

Q6 The world is going to end tomorrow – what do you do?
a) Try to save it, of course!
b) Spend time with the people I love.
c) Check everything's in order for whoever comes along after we've gone.
d) Let's all have sex.
e) It can't possibly end tomorrow! According to my calculations...

Q7 What do you look for in a potential partner?
a) I'm open-minded.
b) Someone loyal, dependable and funny.

SO WHICH MEMBER OF THE TEAM ARE YOU?

MOSTLY a) YOU ARE... CAPTAIN JACK HARKNESS!
Confident, ballsy and always ready for action, you're a born hero through and through. Though it seems like you've got all the time in the world, lazing about and quiet nights in are not your idea of fun! Your practised flirting skills make you the object of many people's affections, and you never find yourself without a date. You're the life and soul of any party, and you have a tale to tell for any occasion. Yet despite your charm and dazzling smile, there's sadness and the weight of responsibility, too. Don't let the pressure or problems from your past keep you awake at night.

MOSTLY b) YOU ARE... GWEN COOPER!
Though you wear your honesty, compassion and caring nature on your sleeve, there's far more to you than meets the eye. Your no-nonsense attitude and ability to empathise with others make you a great friend to have in a crisis, but you've got plenty of emotional dramas of your own! You speak your mind no matter what, and you never stop fighting for what you believe in. Your friends and family are hugely important to you, and you will protect them at any cost. Be careful, though: your feistiness and fervour can sometimes stop you from seeing the bigger picture.

c) Courage, commitment and the capacity to love.
d) Someone passionate, gorgeous – and not necessarily single!
e) Someone who understands me and what I do.

Q8 What scares you?
a) Things I can't change in the past.
b) Losing the people I love.
c) Not being good enough.
d) Death.
e) Not being in control.

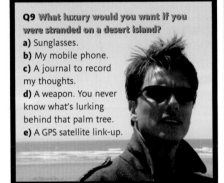

Q9 What luxury would you want if you were stranded on a desert island?
a) Sunglasses.
b) My mobile phone.
c) A journal to record my thoughts.
d) A weapon. You never know what's lurking behind that palm tree.
e) A GPS satellite link-up.

Q10 What do you dream about?
a) I very rarely sleep, so I don't really dream.
b) Starting a family.
c) People I've lost.
d) Things that would make you blush!
e) I usually dream about work.

Q11 What kind of movies do you like?
a) I loved Die Hard 37.
b) Comedies to take my mind off work.
c) Anything black and white does it for me.
d) You can't beat a late night horror film.
e) I actually quite like sci-fi.

Q12 What would be your perfect date?
a) Something unexpected and exciting. Bungee jumping, anyone?
b) Just a whole uninterrupted evening together would be nice.
c) An old movie, then back to mine for coffee?
d) You, me, right here. What do you think? We'd be amazing.
e) Any date at all would be perfect right now.

Q13 What is your best attribute?
a) There are too many to choose from!
b) I never give up.
c) I'm loyal and funny.
d) I'm brilliant!
e) I'm very, very clever.

Q14 And what's your worst?
a) Sometimes, I can seem cold and alien.
b) I can't take no for an answer.
c) I don't always say what I think.
d) I always say what I think!
e) My lack of confidence.

Q15 How do you plan to spend your retirement?
a) I've always wondered what it would be like to be a big old head in a jar. Just kidding!
b) Telling my grandchildren about all the exciting adventures I had when I was young.
c) Running a little antique shop and writing my memoirs, perhaps.
d) Retirement? I intend to live fast and die young, baby!
e) There is so much I want to do, I can't tell you.

Q16 What would you like to be remembered for?
a) Why? I'm not going anywhere.
b) As someone who made a difference.
c) Being utterly indispensable.
d) Just for the really good stuff!
e) Anything except for an incident with the toaster!

MOSTLY c) YOU ARE... IANTO JONES!

You are the most reliable person you know, and you pride yourself on the fact. If something needs doing properly, you do it yourself, and you triple-check it afterwards. Well turned out, good mannered and punctual, don't be surprised if you get taken for granted. Though some may see you as obsessive and introverted, you can be as passionate and unpredictable as the best of them when the situation demands it! Try not to get hung up on past mistakes or your fear of failure – they will only hold you back when courage is required. Rely on your friends and go for it!

MOSTLY d) YOU ARE... OWEN HARPER!

Often swaggering and sarcastic, you use your razor-sharp personality to hide your deepest doubts and fears. You find humour in the darkest places, and inappropriate comments come naturally to you. Be careful: your honesty can be refreshing, but sometimes you just hurt people's feelings! You revel in the sensual pleasures life has to offer, but sooner or later you will have to give up the hedonistic lifestyle. You're clever and compassionate, and deep down you just want to be loved. So why not let your guard down for a bit? The partner of your dreams could be right under your nose!

MOSTLY e) YOU ARE... TOSHIKO SATO!

Work hard, play less, is your motto in life. With a brain like a sponge and a passion to know how things work, you never miss a chance to learn something, and you've always been top of the class. You're quiet and much more caring than you let on, and if people took the time to know you better, they'd realise what a lot of fun you are. You never judge people, and at times you can be a bit too trusting. Other people are the only puzzle you can't solve – but remember some things are better with a bit of mystery. Take some time off! Life's too short.

"

OF EARTH

IN THEIR OWN WORDS

TORCHWOOD: CHILDREN OF EARTH IS THE BIGGEST AND MOST INTENSE ADVENTURE **JOHN BARROWMAN**, **EVE MYLES** AND **GARETH DAVID-LLOYD** HAVE EVER HAD! THEY GOT TOGETHER IN LONDON IN MAY TO TELL THE PRESS ALL ABOUT IT...

EVE MYLES
[GWEN COOPER]

ON THE EVOLUTION OF THE SERIES
"Every year we have to make it better and better, but I still think it's very brave thing to do something so different with a third series. There's more humour this time, but there's more darkness, too. The way the team overcome their obstacles this year is very funny and very cheeky. They break the law, and they do what they have to do to save the world. I think you've got to chuck that humour at the audience to balance out the horror to come, later in the series."

ON BEING GWEN
"She's very clever, and she tends to make people open up. That's a skill Gwen's always had, because she makes them feel comfortable and she's not threatening. She was a fantastic police woman, and that's what Jack needed. That's what she does, and she does it really well – much better than I would be! I'd be absolutely rubbish if the world was ending!"

ON WORKING WITH BIG-NAME GUEST STARS
"I think Paul Copley was my favourite. I adore him in everything he's done, but a couple of months before we started Children Of Earth, I had gone to see him in King Lear at the Globe, and he was just fantastic. I've always admired him and I've always thought he was very underused, and, I have to say, what he did with Clem in this series was amazing. He's brilliant!"

ON BEING PREGNANT
"I've wanted to do this for such a long time, and job after job after job kept coming up, until I just decided that if I put it off any longer I'd be 65 before I said, 'I'm ready now!' I've met some fantastic people who have done just that, but I thought: no that's not happening to me. So we decided this year was going to be the year, and we've been blessed and very lucky that it's happened quite quickly. It's the best thing that's ever happened to me. I'm over the moon."

ON MISSING BURN GORMAN AND NAOKO MORI
"We lost two awesome characters, but more importantly we lost two great friends. But that's the nature of the job, and the nature of Torchwood, and they had amazing stories to go out on. Now they're legends in the world of Torchwood, and huge symbols of how life is short for these characters, and anyone can go. Luckily, they've booked me until I'm 94!"

ON THE FIVE-EPISODE FORMAT
"Telling one story over five hours is a completely different format, but it's completely changed it for the better. My favourite stories in the first two series were the ones that went over two or three episodes, because it's not so rushed. More happens in these five hours than in the 26 that you've seen so far. It's awesome for the characters, and having it all directed by the fantastic Euros Lyn was just amazing."

JOHN BARROWMAN [CAPTAIN JACK]

ON THE EVOLUTION OF THE SERIES
"In series one, we were a newborn learning to crawl, and in series two we were learning to walk. Now we've found our feet and we're running. We still have the alien intervention, but it's more of a straight thriller than ever before – and a lot more frightening, because it's a lot darker, which is what we wanted Torchwood to be in the first place. We tried different things, and now we've finally landed, in a sense."

ON READING THE SCRIPT FOR THE FIRST TIME
"I don't like to interfere with the script. I like to be surprised by the stories, just like everyone else, and that's happened ever since I was first in Doctor Who. Finding out that Jack is the Face of Boe, or that he's got a brother, is what makes it exciting for me to go to work! Jack's always had those different sides to him, and this time you learn about things he's never told anybody. I'm not one of those actors who mulls over things like that: I just get up and do it. But when I come across something new, I do get excited about how I'm going to do it, and how it is going to work."

ON BEING CAPTAIN JACK
"When I'm in that outfit, I am Jack, and when I look at that guy on screen, I see Jack. I'm a huge science fiction fan, so I can take myself out of my reality and put myself into the Torchwood reality very easily. That's why I absolutely love him: because he's someone I'm not."

ON HARD DECISIONS IN CHILDREN OF EARTH
"That's Jack. I've said this from day one: Jack is so determined in his objectives, and his objective is saving the planet. So he is focused, and he is ruthless, and if it means shooting you to stop an alien, then he will shoot you! He'll listen, but if he knows you're lying to him, then boom! You know he's gonna get the alien!"

ON WATCHING CHILDREN OF EARTH
"I will be in Wales watching it on a big-screen television. My family will be over from the States, so we're all going to sit down and make it what it is – proper event television. I'm like a little boy living his fantasy dream!"

ON MISSING BURN GORMAN AND NAOKO MORI
"That's one thing we wanted to make sure that you saw in the show, and why there's a little picture of them in the Hub. They'd been with us since the beginning, and they'll always be a part of Torchwood, even though they're not there physically. Now it's time for a new start, and a new look at the team."

ON THE FIVE-EPISODE FORMAT
"We have to have an event to bring a new audience in, as well as bringing the audience that we already have from BBC2. It's a brilliant piece of television, and it works. Next time I'd like to do even more!"

GARETH DAVID-LLOYD [IANTO JONES]

ON THE EVOLUTION OF THE SERIES
"It's weird, because as an actor you try and develop a backstory to your character, and what we learn about Ianto's home life in this story is almost exactly as I imagined it to be. I grew up on an estate very much like Ianto's, and my sisters still live there, so it was as if Russell had been doing research into my life! So it was really easy to put myself in Ianto's shoes. I think it all rings very true."

ON BEING IANTO
"Ianto was such a mysterious character, originally. You didn't know where he was from or what made him tick. He was kind of the comedy relief, but now that's been put into perspective, and you see that the dryness and the quips are to hide his insecurities and his fears. He uses comedy to hide his more sensitive and vulnerable side, and those two elements have married quite well this series."

ON NOT BEING IANTO
"At conventions people are quite taken aback, because they're expecting this stilted, dark, emotional young man in a suit – and then I turn up in a hoodie, with a scruffy beard, playing heavy metal music! A lot of the fans have got to know me now, though, and I think they enjoy the difference. And it helps not being recognised in the street –because I'm actually a scruffy git!"

ON PORTRAYING A GAY MAN ON BBC1
"I think it's great. A lot of shows are made about being gay, where you have gay couples at the forefront and everything is an 'issue', but with this, the normality of having a gay relationship is an important part of the show. It's not pushed in your face or anything: it's just there. I think that's quite important."

ON MISSING BURN GORMAN AND NAOKO MORI
"I think that we, as actors, were missing Burn and Naoko just as much as our characters were missing Owen and Tosh. But the great thing about it is that none of the characters are safe. Big tragedies can happen to people in the sci-fi world, just as easily as they can to people in single-camera slice-of-life dramas. That's what makes the scary bits scary – because you see these characters in domestic situations, and you recognise yourself in them."

ON THE FIVE-EPISODE FORMAT
"When they first said it was going to be five episodes I was a bit put out, because I was expecting more work! But then I got the scripts and realised it was going to be one long story, which actually took the pressure off, in the sense that we haven't got two or three storylines in our heads all at once. That meant we were able to do this story more organically from beginning to end. I think I'm more proud of it than anything we've done before."

THE CREATURE FROM THE 13TH FLOOR!

WHAT ALIEN TERRORS LURK BEHIND THE HEAVILY GUARDED DOORS OF FLOOR 13 IN **TORCHWOOD: CHILDREN OF EARTH?** WE TOOK AN EXCLUSIVE TRIP ON SET TO INVESTIGATE...

Day 70 on the set of Torchwood: Children Of Earth, and it looks set to be a day of lasts, biggests, snots and vomit. Mmm... Vomit. The first last (as it were) is that this is the last day of Children Of Earth scheduled to be filmed at Cardiff's Upper Boat studios, and the two biggests are the set itself, and the studio in which it is standing.

The venue of choice is studio six – reserved for some of the largest and the most important sets on Torchwood and Doctor Who. For fact fans out there, studio six has played host to both of the last two Doctor Who finales, having been the Dalek Crucible from where Davros tried to detonate his Reality Bomb in The Stolen Earth/Journey's End, and the Valiant from where the Master decimated

the world's population in The Sound Of Drums/The Last Of The Time Lords. It's fair to say that if an alien or a megalomaniac (or even a megalomaniac alien) is going to plot against humanity, they'd be wise to do it from studio six – and today is no exception.

The set is known as Floor 13, an ominous title that suggests whatever goes on here is not going to be good news for anyone. However, standby art director Arwel Wyn Jones doesn't seem superstitious about the name, and enthuses about Floor 13 at every opportunity.

"It's huge!" he says. "I'm so proud of it. It's definitely my favourite set." Coming from a man who has been on the design team of Doctor Who since the early days of the Russell T Davies era, that's saying quite a lot!

It's not hard to see what he means, either. Floor 13 is the largest set ever constructed for Torchwood or Doctor Who at Upper Boat (before you ask, both The Hub and the TARDIS interior were built partially or completely off site, but Floor 13 was built right here). It's so large, the entire crew is packed into one corner of the remaining studio space, jostling for position with monitors and equipment.

At the heart of Floor 13 is a large glass vault filled with gas. Plenty of key scenes for Children Of Earth will take place around this cabinet, and every character will be in some way affected by what's inside it. Because this isn't some over-sized icebox filled with lunch for a hungry cast and crew. This is the secret of Floor 13. This is the home of new Torchwood aliens, the 456...

"FLOOR 13 IS THE LARGEST SET EVER CONSTRUCTED FOR TORCHWOOD OR DOCTOR WHO AT UPPER BOAT. AT ITS HEART IS A LARGE GLASS VAULT..."

Now, there's obviously not much we can say about the 456 without spoiling the surprise, but we can tell you it's been created by Neill Gorton's team at Millennium FX and – like the floor on which it lives – it is one of the largest and most ambitious creatures ever created for either Torchwood or Doctor Who. Children Of Earth writer and executive producer Russell T Davies knew what he wanted from the 456 all along, and briefed Millennium FX before he'd even finished writing the first script, so the team had as much time as possible to design and build the creature. Now, five months later, the results of all that forward planning really are a sight to behold...

More than seven feet high, and requiring five people to operate it (three in front and two behind, all communicating via headphones and radios), the 456 is a feat of engineering. The operating team themselves have the attractive title of 'snotters', thanks to their secondary task of regularly coating the creature in clear stringy mucus, making sure it keeps dripping from every angle. Shooting is regularly halted by a cry of "Can we re-snot the 456?" and in trot the snotters, ready to throw on more gunk at a moment's notice. There: we hope that hasn't spoiled anything for you...

With the 456 fully snotted-up, filming is ready to begin. But when the call for total quiet comes, it's not an easy thing to achieve. Not only is the Upper Boat complex a former factory next to a railway line, but (like any other studio) it is also plagued by all the tiny noises you'd never notice anywhere else. Every chair seems to creak a little louder and each stomach rumble seems to last a little longer whenever you're on a set, but, ▶

as everyone settles for rehearsal prior to a take, a certain hush is achieved. Well, until a rogue vacuum cleaner starts up in the props store next door, that is. The vacuum cleaner and its operator are soon silenced by a runner (yes, that is meant to sound a little sinister: runners can be very scary people at times), and the scene is ready to begin.

It's a scene that marks another of the day's lasts, as it sees Torchwood's best dressed operative, Ianto Jones, uttering his last lines for this series, with the completion of a sequence that was begun last night. In fact, several characters are about to film their last scenes today, as – though there is still a week of filming left to go – the scenes are not shot in transmission order, and some of the later scenes were shot relatively early on. Gareth David-Lloyd completes the scene with aplomb, then celebrates with a cheer of "No more lines!" before running to his trailer to fling off his character's smart suit in favour of much more casual jeans and a T-shirt.

Next to perform his final scene in Children Of Earth is Ian Gelder, who plays the likeably unlikeable Dekker. At nearly two pages, the scene is the longest of the day – and while that might not sound like much, it's an eternity in TV terms, and represents a significant chunk of the working day. Today the team will tackle six pages in all, which will result in about 10 minutes of screen time, but it will take 11 hours to get it right. So it's not surprising that once Dekker's last scene is completed, there's a sense of achievement and relief, and a round of applause for the departing actor (and possibly because it's time for lunch).

After lunch, shooting recommences with Charles Abomeli (Colonel Oduya) taking centre stage on Floor 13. But, as the afternoon is getting underway, another interruption, more pleasant than a hoover, occurs as executive producers Julie Gardner and Russell T Davies arrive on set. Though they've dropped by to see the 456 in action, conversation quickly turns to the first Doctor Who special of 2009, Planet Of The Dead, which is still five months away at this point. The excitement is palpable, especially when the word "Dubai" is mentioned. But before Russell can give too much away, Julie tells him: "Right! We're going. We're distracting them and you've got more writing to do!" She's right, of course, and with that they're gone: off to plot for the future...

As filming continues, a problem is noticed with vomit. The tension hasn't made any one sick – rather someone has thrown away the vomit needed for this afternoon's scenes. Suddenly, there is an urgent need for sick. Unfortunately, lunch was as good as always, so no one's feeling productive in that sense, but the Any Effects team (better known for explosions of another sort) are on the case and mixing it up. "Henry, can you do three different colours of vomit?" goes the cry. "No problem," comes the reply. All told, it looks like being a very pleasant afternoon...

While various substances are mixed outside, shooting continues without interruptions, and director Euros Lyn is positioning a team of extras, dressed as UNIT soldiers around the perimeter of Floor 13. It's a difficult scene, and getting things to look right on camera is proving tricky. Calling over his radio to first assistant director Steffan Morris, Euros asks, "Could the soldier on the right be a bit more upright? You know, like a soldier?" Direction received, the soldier straightens up and

filming continues. Steffan reads in the actions of the 456, to help guide both Millennium FX and Colonel Oduya's reactions, and is advised to be as dramatic as he wants – leading to a very impressive performance indeed.

As more scenes are slowly ticked off, the multicoloured vomit comes into play, splattered against a screen in a suitably revolting manner. To ensure that the team gets the perfect shot, the buckets are refilled and another batch is liberally sprayed. A quick check of, "Is there any more vomit?" elicits a, "No, all puked out," and so it's time to move on to the final scene.

Before long, three SAs (supporting actors) arrive on set suspiciously soon after the arrival of some really rich cream cakes, but they assure us there's no connection. That comes as a relief when another SA appears wearing a biohazard suit, as several of the cakes have been eaten already, and no one wants to help replenish the vomit stock... One of the other SAs whispers gleefully, " I get to help him out of that bio-suit in a bit. He's only got pants on underneath!" She thinks about this for a moment, and then adds, "Do you think I should have warmed my hands up?"

Of course, the last scene of the day wouldn't be complete without an interruption all its own, so just as things are getting

underway, a problem arises that threatens not only the day's production but the entire rest of the shoot: someone has forgotten who they picked for Secret Santa! It must be serious, as associate producer Catrin Defis has arrived on set and is working up a plan of action with runners Nicola Brown and Alison 'Blodwyn' Jones.

"Someone – I won't say who," Catrin tells us with a sigh, "has forgotten whose name they

Ian Gelder as Dekker.

THE CREATURE FROM THE 13TH FLOOR!

drew, and it turns out no one made a list. If we don't find out, someone's going to be without a present!"

It's hard to deny the scale of the dilemma, so Nicola and Ali hand out fresh pieces of paper to everyone, so they can write down who they've picked in the mutual gift-giving scheme, and find out who's left over. Euros insists on doing his under cover – waving his pen around so that no one can work it out from his pen movements.

With the day's final scene in the can, and the Secret Santa situation under control, Torchwood magazine is ready to depart. With all the snot that's been flying around, we can't help but suggest that whoever gets the 456 in the Secret Santa might want to consider the excellent range of Doctor Who handkerchiefs now available, but apparently animatronic aliens aren't eligible.

On that note, we step off the biggest set at Upper Boat for the last time (on Children Of Earth, at least). As we take one last look at the day's call sheet, we wonder what nugget of information we can share with the readers of Torchwood Magazine to whet their appetite for what's to come. The obvious choice is the description of that very last scene of the day – a moment which more than justifies the three dots at the end of it: "The soldier sees the horrible truth..."

Of course, to find out what that might be, you'll just have to tune in to Children Of Earth. But rest assured, the secrets of Floor 13 are much worse than not getting a Secret Santa present! T

Charles Abomeli as Colonel Oduya.

"WHILE VARIOUS SUBSTANCES ARE MIXED OUTSIDE, DIRECTOR EUROS LYN IS POSITIONING A TEAM OF EXTRAS, DRESSED AS UNIT SOLDIERS..."

TORCHWOOD

THE OFFICIAL MAGAZINE YEARBOOK

ISBN: 9781848562394

Published by Titan Books
A division of Titan Publishing Group Ltd
144 Southwark St London SE1 0UP

First edition September 2009
10 9 8 7 6 5 4 3 2 1

BBC and Torchwood (word marks and logos) and the Torchwood symbol are trade marks of the British Broadcasting Corporation and are used under licence. BBC logo © BBC 1996. Torchwood logo © BBC 2006. Torchwood symbol © BBC 2006. Series created by Russell T Davies. Licensed by BBC Worldwide Limited.

Visit our website: www.titanbooks.com

A CIP catalogue record for this title is available from the British Library.

Printed and bound in Italy.

Acknowledgements: Titan Books would like to thank the cast and crew of Torchwood who gave up their valuable time for the interviews included in this book. Thanks also to Gary Russell and David Turbitt at the BBC. Many thanks to designer Philip White and editor Simon Hugo at Torchwood Magazine. And, for their contributions to this book, thanks must also go to Kate Anderson (pp80-83), Neil Edwards (74-79), Sarah Herman (13-15, 20-29, 37-39, 40-44, 57-59, 60-67, 80-83), Simon Hugo (16-19) and Matt Nicholls (90-93).